Astron

Notebooking Journal

for

Exploring Creation with Astronomy

by
Jeannie Fulbright

Astronomy Notebooking Journal

Published by
Apologia Educational Ministries, Inc.
1106 Meridian Plaza, Suite 220
Anderson, IN 46016

www.apologia.com

Manufactured in the United States of America
First Printing 2009

ISBN: 978-1-932012-94-1

Printed by Courier Printing, Kendallville, IN

Cover photos courtesy NASA/JPL/Caltech

Cover Design by Kim Williams

All Biblical Quotations are from the New American Standard Bible, New King James Version, King James Version.

Photo Credits

NASA.gov: Cover, pp. 9, 15, 26, 27, 31, 35, 39, 44, 51, 57, 61, 63, 66, 67, 71, 75, 78, 84, 85, 89, 90, 94, 95, 105, 09, 115, 120, 119, 125, 134, 135, 140, 145, v, vii, ix, xvii, xxv, xxix, xxxii, xxxv, xli xlv, xlvii, xlix, li, liii, lix lxi

Crestock Images: 41, 55, 139 & lv (astronaut), i, xxvii (scale)

Brad Fitzpatrick Images: 19, 20, 21, 22, xi, xxi, xxiii, xxxviii

Angie Coleman of Artistic Energy: xix

All other images licensed from Jupiter Images.

Font Credits

Fonts used with permission/license from:

David Rakowski - Starburst
P22 Foundry, Inc. - LTC Fourneir
Font Diner: Starburst Lanes Twinkle, Bingo, FontDinerDotCom Sparkely, Black Night, Spacearella, Hothead, Mirage Zanzibar
Educational Fontware, Inc - HWT
John Stracke- Rockets
Brian Ether - Orbitronio
My Fonts.com: Astype - Alea, Intellecta Design - Ulma, Bailarina, Worm, Gavinha, Half Flower, Wundes - Sprouts, Wiescher Desgin - Barracuda, Vivian, TypeSetit - FleurDeLeah, Bomparte - Black Swan, Scriptorium - Morris Inhas, Mandragora, Nick's Fonts - HarvestMoon, Otto Maurer - Hotrod, Arttypes - Maria Belle, Studiocharlie - Super Starlike, HiH Retrofonts - Waltari, Gradl, Aah Yes - Starbell Two, FontHaus - Novella, BitStream, Inc

Note from the Author

Welcome to the wonderful adventure in learning called "Notebooking." This notebooking journal correlates with Apologia's *Exploring Creation with Astronomy*, by Jeannie Fulbright. The activities in this journal provide everything your child needs to complete the assignments in *Exploring Creation with Astronomy* and more. It will serve as your child's individual notebook. You only need to provide scissors, glue, colored pencils, a stapler and some brass fasteners.

The concept of notebooking is not a new one. In fact, keeping notebooks was the primary way the learned men of our past educated themselves, from Leonardo Da Vinci and Christopher Columbus to George Washington, John Quincy Adams and Meriwether Lewis. These men and many others of their time were avid notebookers. As we know, they were also much more advanced in their knowledge—even as teens—than we are today. George Washington was a licensed surveyor during his teenage years, and John Quincy Adams graduated from law school at age 17.

It would be wise for us to emulate the methods of education of these great men, rather than the failing methods used in our schools today. Common modern methods, namely fill-in-the-blank and matching worksheets, do not fully engage the student's mind. Studies show that we remember only 5% of what we hear, 50% of what we see and hear and 90% of what we see, hear and do. When we participate in activities that correspond with learning, we increase our retention exponentially. This is exactly what the Astronomy Notebooking Journal is designed to do—offer engaging learning activities to increase your student's retention.

The National Center for Educational Statistics shows us that American school children, by twelfth grade, rank at the bottom of international assessments, and do not even know 50% of what students in top ranked countries know. As home educators, we have the opportunity to discard methods that are detrimental and ineffective, and adopt the methods which will genuinely educate our children.

In addition to academic achievement, notebooking offers many benefits to students and parents. For students, it provides an opportunity to uniquely express themselves as they learn. It also provides a treasured memento of educational endeavors. For parents, it is a record of the year's studies and can easily be transferred to a portfolio if needed.

This journal will make notebooking easier for both you and your student by supplying a plethora of templates, hands-on crafts and projects, additional experiment ideas, and many activities that will engage your student in learning. It will prove invaluable in helping students create a wonderful keepsake of all they learned in astronomy. Remember that everything in this notebooking journal is optional. Because it will serve as your student's own unique notebook, you may customize it by simply tearing out the activity pages that you choose not to use. You, as the teacher, will decide what truly benefits your student's learning experience, encourages a love for learning and builds his confidence in science. Every child is different, learns differently and will respond differently to the array of activities provided here. Use discernment in how many of the activities and assignments you use with your child. Your goal is not to complete every activity, but to make learning a joy.

However, as a seasoned home educator, let me encourage you not to attempt to do every single activity in this notebooking journal. Choose the projects and activities that will be enjoyable and inspire a love of learning. If something is a drudgery, it will not serve to increase your student's retention, but will only discourage their enjoyment of science—resulting in an unmotivated learner.

It is my hope and prayer that you and your students will benefit from your studies this year, growing closer to God as you learn of His creation, and finding joy in the learning process.

Warmly,

Jeannie Fulbright

Astronomy Notebooking Journal

Below are descriptions of a suggested schedule and the activities included in this notebooking journal. The first three activities are taken directly from the coursework contained in *Exploring Creation with Astronomy*. The others are additional optional activities coordinating with the book.

Suggested Schedule

A suggested schedule for reading the *Exploring Creation with Astronomy* text and completing the activities contained in the book and in this journal has been provided. Though not every student or parent will choose to utilize the schedule, those who do may find it very beneficial. Some parents will appreciate having their student's daily reading and assignments organized for them. Older students will find it easy to complete the book and journal by following the schedule on their own. Though the suggested schedule provides for the astronomy course to be completed in twenty-eight weeks, two days per week, it is flexible and can be made to fit your goals. The course can be expedited by completing three or four days of science per week. You can lengthen the course by studying science only one day per week. If you wish to do the extra activities found in the Take It Further pages, still another day of science can be added. Above all, use the suggested schedule in a way that best suits your family.

Fascinating Facts

Exploring Creation with Astronomy contains many facts, ideas and interesting notions. Although oral (verbal) narration is an effective means for retention, your student may wish to record some of the information either through drawing or writing. The Fascinating Facts pages can be used for written narrations. Some of the lessons provide two Fascinating Facts pages for our student's use. If your student is an avid writer, you can access more Fascinating Facts pages to print (free of charge) on the Apologia website. To do so, simply login to www.apologia.com/bookextras and type in this password: Godcreateditall. These additional pages can be included in this notebooking journal by simply stapling them onto one of the existing Fascinating Facts pages.

What Do You Remember? Review Questions

These review questions are the same questions asked in the "What Do You Remember?" section found in each chapter of the book. They can be answered orally (verbally) or, for older students, as a written narration assignment. For co-ops or classroom use, these questions may also serve as a way to evaluate how much the students have retained from the reading. However, I would encourage you to review the material with the students before giving the questions as a written narration assignment. This will encourage better retention of the material and increase both the students' confidence and their ability to restate their learning. The answers to the review questions can be found on page 173 through 175 of *Exploring Creation with Astronomy.*

Notebook Assignments, Activities and Projects

The lessons in *Exploring Creation with Astronomy* offer suggested notebook assignments, activities and projects typically found at the end of each lesson. Provided in this journal are templates (blank pages with lines for writing or space for drawing) which your student can use for completing these activities. Most often the assignment is to create or illustrate a cover page for that lesson. Colored pencils can be used to encourage creative, high quality work.

Scripture Copywork

Incorporating the Word of God in your science studies through Scripture copywork will provide many benefits to your student. It will encourage stronger faith and memorization of Scripture, as well as better writing, spelling and grammar skills. Each lesson has a corresponding verse for your child to copy, which may be printed or written in cursive.

Vocabulary Crosswords

If you desire to expand your child's studies with vocabulary activities, the Vocabulary Crosswords can be used to review the new words and concepts mentioned in the chapter. Remember, working with the vocabulary in this manner is not a "test" of your child's knowledge, but should be viewed as a reinforcement and reminder of what he has learned. The answers to the Vocabulary Crosswords can be found on pages 153 and 154.

Project Pages

Many of the projects and experiments in *Exploring Creation with Astronomy* are "hands-on" and therefore cannot be preserved in a notebook. Each lesson in this notebooking journal provides a Project Page in which your student can write about what he did and learned from the various projects and experiments contained in the coursework. Be sure to take pictures of the finished products and glue them onto the Project Pages. Your child will enjoy looking back and remembering the fun he had learning astronomy!

Cut and Fold Miniature Books

At the back of this journal, you will find Cut and Fold Miniature Book educational activities that correspond with the reading. These miniature books are designed to assist the students' review and retention of the concepts learned in each lesson. They also provide a record of the course work performed. Students will cut out the pattern, write what they have learned in the designated places, then assemble the books according to the directions. Paste Pages are included for each miniature book activity. The Paste Pages provide a place for your students to preserve and display their Cut and Fold Miniature Books. Instructions are included for pasting the miniature books onto the Paste Pages.

However, these books are entirely optional, and you can decide whether or not to allow your student to utilize these miniature books.

Take It Further

The Take It Further assignments are designed to give your student additional ideas and activities that might enhance his studies such as: experiments, hands-on activities, research and living book titles, as well as audio and video resources. Because these assignments are entirely optional, they are not included in the suggested schedule for completing the notebooking journal.

Field Trip Sheets

Your family may wish to further enhance your studies by visiting a planetarium or space museum. You can also spend an evening with the local astronomy club to view the planets through their powerful telescopes. Field Trip Sheets are provided at the back of this notebooking journal to record your visits. You can make a pocket on the back of these sheets to hold any brochures or additional information you receive. Simply glue three edges (sides and bottom) of a half piece of construction paper to the bottom of the field trip sheet.

Final Review

At the end of this journal are 50 questions that review the entire course. They can be answered orally or in writing. This is an optional activity; however, I believe your students would be pleasantly surprised to see how much they know about astronomy after answering the questions. The answers to the Final Review can be found on page 155.

Table of Contents

Table of Contents

Week:	Day 1	Day 2
1	**Lesson 1 - What is Astronomy?** Read pp. 2-5 & Narrate Begin working on ***Fascinating Facts***	Read pp. 5-8 & Narrate Narration: ***What Do You Remember? Review Questions*** Notebook Assignment: ***Illustrate a Cover Page***
2	**Lesson 1 - What is Astronomy?** Notebook Assignment: ***Mnemonic*** ***Scripture Copywork***	***Vocabulary Crossword*** Project: ***Solar System*** pp. 9-10 ***Cut and Fold Miniature Books***
3	**Lesson 2 - The Sun** Read pp. 12-17 & Narrate Answer questions on pp. 14 & 16 & Narrate Begin working on ***Fascinating Facts***	Read pp. 18-19 Mid-lesson Activity: ***Illustrate a Cover Page*** Mid-lesson Activity: ***Write a Speech***
4	**Lesson 2 - The Sun** Read pp. 20-25 & Narrate Answer question on p. 22 Narration: ***What Do You Remember? Review Questions*** Notebook Assignment: ***Sun Collage*** ***Scripture Copywork***	***Vocabulary Crossword*** Activity: ***Make a Solar Eclipse*** p. 26 Project: ***Pinhole Viewing Box*** pp. 27-28 ***Cut and Fold Miniature Books***
5	**Lesson 3 - Mercury** Read pp. 30-34 & Narrate Answer question on p. 32 & Narrate Begin working on ***Fascinating Facts***	Read pp. 34-36 & Narrate Narration: ***What Do You Remember? Review Questions*** Notebook Assignment: ***Illustrate a Cover Page***
6	**Lesson 3 - Mercury** Activity: Craters p. 37 ***Scripture Copywork***	***Vocabulary Crossword*** Project: ***Make a Model of Mercury*** p. 38 ***Cut and Fold Miniature Books***
7	**Lesson 4 - Venus** Read pp. 40-41 & Narrate Do Mid-lesson Activity p. 41 Begin working on ***Fascinating Facts***	Read pp. 42-47 & Narrate Narration: ***What Do You Remember? Review Questions***
8	**Lesson 4 - Venus** Notebook Assignment: ***Illustrate a Cover Page*** Notebook Activity: ***Comic Strip*** ***Scripture Copywork***	***Vocabulary Crossword*** Project: ***Learn How Radar is Used*** p. 49 ***Cut and Fold Miniature Books***
9	**Lesson 5 - Earth** Read pp. 52-57 & Narrate Begin working on ***Fascinating Facts***	Read pp. 57- 63 & Narrate Narration: ***What Do You Remember? Review Questions***
10	**Lesson 5 - Earth** Notebook Assignment: ***Illustrate a Cover Page*** Notebook Activity: ***Advertisement*** ***Scripture Copywork***	***Vocabulary Crossword*** Project: ***Make a Compass*** p. 64 ***Cut and Fold Miniature Books***
11	**Lesson 6 - Moon** Read pp. 66-70 & Narrate Begin working on ***Fascinating Facts***	Read pp. 70-74 & Narrate Narration: ***What Do You Remember? Review Questions***
12	**Lesson 6 - Moon** Notebook Assignment: ***Illustrate a Cover Page*** Notebook Activity: ***Moon Phase Chart*** ***Scripture Copywork***	***Vocabulary Crossword*** Project: ***Make a Telescope*** pp. 75-76 ***Cut and Fold Miniature Books***
13	**Lesson 7 - Mars** Read pp. 78- 82 & Narrate Begin working on ***Fascinating Facts***	Read pp. 82- 85 & Narrate Narration: ***What Do You Remember? Review Questions***
14	**Lesson 7 - Mars** Notebook Assignment: ***Illustrate a Cover Page*** ***Scripture Copywork***	***Vocabulary Crossword*** Project: ***Build Olympus Mons*** pp. 87- 88 ***Cut and Fold Miniature Books***

Week:	Day 1	Day 2
15	**Lesson 8 - Space Rocks** Read pp. 90-94 & Narrate Answer questions on p. 93 Begin working on ***Fascinating Facts***	Read pp. 95-99 & Narrate Narration: ***What Do You Remember? Review Questions***
16	**Lesson 8 - Space Rocks** Notebook Assignment: ***Illustrate a Cover Page*** Notebook Assignment: ***Meteor Showers*** ***Scripture Copywork***	***Vocabulary Crossword*** Project: ***Create a Scale Model Solar System*** pp. 101-102 ***Cut and Fold Miniature Books***
17	**Lesson 9 - Jupiter** Read pp. 104-106 & Narrate Begin working on ***Fascinating Facts***	Read pp. 107-110 & Narrate Narration: ***What Do You Remember? Review Questions***
18	**Lesson 9 - Jupiter** Notebook Assignment: ***Make a Newspaper*** ***Scripture Copywork***	***Vocabulary Crossword*** Project: ***Make a Hurricane Tube*** p.112 ***Cut and Fold Miniature Books***
19	**Lesson 10 - Saturn** Read pp. 114-118 & Narrate Begin working on ***Fascinating Facts***	Narration: ***What Do You Remember? Review Questions***
20	**Lesson 10 - Saturn** Notebook Assignment: ***Illustrate a Cover Page*** Notebook Assignment: ***Make a Venn Diagram*** ***Scripture Copywork***	***Vocabulary Crossword*** Project: ***Make a Centaur Rocket*** pp. 119-120 ***Cut and Fold Miniature Books***
21	**Lesson 11 - Uranus & Neptune** Read pp. 122-124 & Narrate Begin working on ***Fascinating Facts*** Narration: ***What Do You Remember? Review Questions Uranus***	Read pp. 125-127 & Narrate Narration: ***What Do You Remember? Review Questions Neptune***
22	**Lesson 11 - Uranus & Neptune** Notebook Assignment: ***Illustrate a Cover Page*** ***Scripture Copywork***	***Vocabulary Crossword*** Project: ***Make Clouds*** p. 130 ***Cut and Fold Miniature Books***
23	**Lesson 12 - Pluto & Kuiper Belt** Read pp. 132-135 & Narrate Begin working on ***Fascinating Facts***	Read pp. 136-138 & Narrate Narration: ***What Do You Remember? Review Questions***
24	**Lesson 12 - Pluto & Kuiper Belt** Notebook Assignment: ***Illustrate a Cover Page*** Notebook Assignment: ***Pluto Debate*** ***Scripture Copywork***	***Vocabulary Crossword*** Project: ***Make Ice Cream!*** p. 140 ***Cut and Fold Miniature Books***
25	**Lesson 13 - Stars & Galaxies** Read pp. 142-148 & Narrate Begin working on ***Fascinating Facts***	Read pp. 149-155 & Narrate Narration: ***What Do You Remember? Review Questions***
26	**Lesson 13 - Stars & Galaxies** Notebook Assignment: ***Illustrate a Cover Page*** ***Scripture Copywork***	***Vocabulary Crossword*** Project: ***Make an Astrometer*** p. 157 Project: ***Create a Constellation Planetarium*** p. 158 ***Cut and Fold Miniature Books***
27	**Lesson 14 - Space Travel** Read pp. 160-167 & Narrate Begin working on ***Fascinating Facts***	Read pp. 167-169 & Narrate Narration: ***What Do You Remember? Review Questions***
28	**Lesson 14 - Space Travel** Notebook Assignment: ***Illustrate a Cover Page*** Notebook Activity: ***Let's Visit the Planets!*** ***Scripture Copywork***	***Vocabulary Crossword*** Project: ***Build a Model Space Station*** p. 172 ***Cut and Fold Miniature Books***

This Notebook Belongs to:
Sarah Green

FASCINATING FACTS ABOUT Astronomy

Name ____ Date ________________

What Do You Remember?
Lesson 1 Review Questions

1. Why did God create the stars and planets?

2. What are the names of the planets?

3. What is the name of America's space program?

4. What does NASA do?

5. Which astronomer first said the earth revolves around the sun?

6. Who learned how to study space with a telescope?

Astronomy

Mnemonic

Mnemonic with Pluto

Mercury	Venus	Earth	Mars	Jupiter	Saturn	Uranus	Neptune	Pluto

Write Your Sentence Here:

____

____

Mnemonic without Pluto

Mercury	Venus	Earth	Mars	Jupiter	Saturn	Uranus	Neptune

Write Your Sentence Here:

____

____

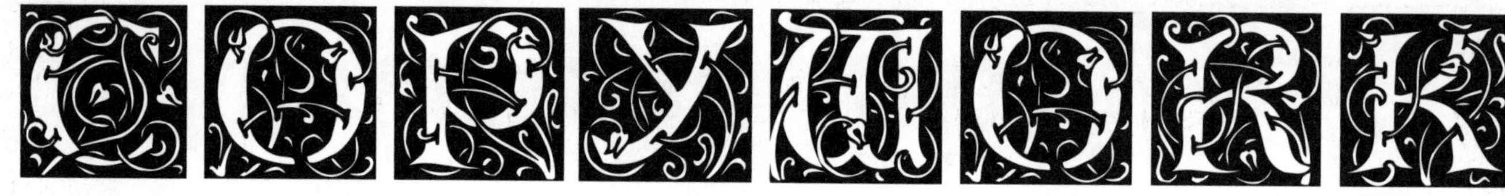

The heavens are telling of the glory of God; and their expanse is declaring the work of His hands. Psalm 19:1

The heavens are telling of the glory of God; and their expanse is declaring the work of His hands. Psalm 19:1

Vocabulary Crossword

Lesson 1

NASA

GALILEO

COPERNICUS

INSTINCT

UNIVERSE

STONEHENGE

GRAVITY

Across

1. America's space agency, called the National Aeronautics and Space Administration.
3. A scientist who built telescopes and studied astronomy.
6. A special gift God gives to creatures, causing them to behave in a certain manner that is helpful to their survival, such as with birds flying south for the winter.
7. A scientist who discovered that the earth revolves around the sun, rather than the sun revolving around the earth, as was believed at the time.

Down

2. An ancient monument in England that may have been used to predict the arrival of spring and other seasons.
4. A physical force causing objects to pull on other objects, such as with the sun pulling on the earth.
5. Everything that exists in space, including the earth, planets, sun, and stars.

My Astronomy Project

What I did:

What I learned:

What is Astronomy?

TAKE IT FURTHER

LESSON 1

Hanging Solar System in a Box

You will need:
Clay
Thread
A copy paper box (found at office supply stores)
A sharp pencil
Duct tape (or other strong tape)

Using the sizes for the planets on page 10 of *Exploring Creation with Astronomy*, you can create a smaller scale solar system using clay. Simply reduce the sizes to millimeters or centimeters and model each planet out of clay, forming balls. If you are not worried about making it perfectly to scale, you can make the smaller planets a little larger for ease of handling. You will want to insert a piece of thread in the center of each planet before it dries, using a threaded needle. Hang the planets inside the box by using the sharp pencil to make holes in the top of the box, inserting the free ends of the thread through the holes and taping them down with duct tape.

Solar System Mobile

You will need:
Cardstock
Colored markers
Tacks
String
Tape

An even simpler idea is to create a solar system mobile using cardstock and markers. Reduce the sizes on page 10 of *Exploring Creation with Astronomy* to centimeters and draw circles on the cardstock to represent each planet. For larger planets, you will need to piece two pages together. Color the planets and cut them out (or use colored construction paper). Tape the string to them and tack the paper planets to the ceiling as you would the balloons.

Make a Model of Stonehenge

Make a model of Stonehenge with clay. Look at pictures on the Internet to see how it is formed from different perspectives. Be sure to photograph it for your Astronomy Project Page!

Books

Along Came Galileo by Jeanne Bendick
Starry Messenger by Peter Sis
Nicolaus Copernicus: The Earth Is a Planet by Dennis Fradin
Signs and Seasons by Jay Ryan

Audio CD

Galileo and the Stargazers by Jim Weiss

Fascinating Facts

about

The Sun

FASCINATING FACTS

ABOUT

THE SUN

SUN

Why You Should not
Look at the
SUN

Name ______________________________ Date ______________

What Do You Remember?
Lesson 2 Review Questions

1. How many earths would fit inside the sun?

2. How many miles away is the sun? (circle your answer)

   a. 92,957 b. 92,935 c. 92,935,700 d. 97,935,200

3. What is the solar system?

4. What are sunspots and how do they affect the earth?

5. Does the sun have a satellite?

6. What is the difference between revolving and rotating?

7. How does the sun tell us that there were not living things on the earth billions of years ago?

8. Why do we see color?

9. Which color has short waves?

10. What is a solar eclipse?

SUN COLLAGE

From the rising of the sun unto the going down of the same the LORD's name is to be praised. Psalm 113:3

From the rising of the sun unto the going down of the same the LORD's name is to be praised. Psalm 113:3

Vocabulary Crossword

Lesson 2

1 2 3 4 5 6 7 8 9 10 11 12 13

Vocabulary Crossword

Lesson 2

ROTATE
AURORAS
REVOLVE
THERMONUCLEAR FUSION
PARTIAL ECLIPSE
ORBIT
BAILEY'S BEADS
TOTAL ECLIPSE
SOLAR FLARES
DROUGHTS
SUNSPOTS
ATMOSPHERE
ANNULAR ECLIPSE

Across

2. This occurs when the moon is between the earth and the sun, completely covering the sun, causing the moon to cast a shadow upon the earth **(put a space between the two words)**.
4. Long seasons of extremely dry weather with no rain, which can be caused by too many sun spots.
6. The path that an object in space (such as a planet, moon, or satellite) follows around a larger object in space, such as the Sun.
7. These are small points of sunlight that can be seen around the moon during an eclipse. This happens because the moon is not a perfectly round ball, but has many irregularities and craters **(put a space between the two words)**.
10. The layers of gases and mist that cover a planet, such as the earth.
11. To orbit, or move in a circular motion around another object. An object that orbits another object is said to __________ around that object.
12. An eclipse that displays a ring of sunlight around the moon. This happens when the moon is farther away from the earth **(put a space between the two words)**.
13. Nuclear reactions (controlled explosions) occurring on the sun that give it energy and power **(put a space between the two words)**.

Down

1. Large fires which burst out millions of miles from the sun, releasing energy into the solar system **(put a space between the two words)**.
3. A solar eclipse that occurs when the moon is not directly between the sun and the earth **(put a space between the two words).**
5. Dark patches upon the sun which are cooler than the rest of the sun.
8. Natural, colorful light displays in the sky that can be caused by solar flares.
9. To turn around a fixed point, such as how a top spins in place or a planet spins on its axis.

What I did:

What I learned:

THE SUN

TAKE IT FURTHER

LESSON 2

Learn about Shadows and the Sun

You will need:
A dowel
Your yard
A sunny day
Measuring tape

You can learn about the way the shadows change throughout the day. On a sunny day, in the early morning, place a dowel in the ground and measure the length of the shadow, noting the time and where the shadow falls in relation to the sun and the earth. Every few hours, go outside and measure the shadow, noting the time. You can create a simple chart with the time and length of the shadow. This will be a tool you can use to record your observations.

Purchase Solar Glasses

You can purchase solar glasses with which to view the sun directly. One can see sun spots and solar flares through these glasses. They are the only safe glasses to use when looking at the sun. Never look at the sun without special devices made for this purpose. To find them on the Internet, use the search term, "eclipse glasses."

Learn about Color

You will need:
A coffee filter
A water-based black marker
A cup of rubbing alcohol

This experiment will help you see that black is all the colors of the rainbow mixed together. Fold a coffee filter in half, creating a half circle. Draw a thick line in an arch just below the ruffled edge, creating a black rainbow shape on your coffee filter. Fold the coffee filter in half again, making a pizza slice shape. Put the pointed end in a cup of alcohol, keeping the black arch above the alcohol line. As the alcohol absorbs into the filter, it will spread up to the black arch and begin to separate the colors.

Solar Prints

Place various objects (scissors, rubber bands, pencils) on a piece of blue and a piece of red construction paper, and place the papers in a sunny spot outside. At the end of the day, remove the objects. What caused the paper to fade around the objects? Which paper faded more? Why do you think that is, based on what you learned about color and the sun?

Fascinating Facts

About

Mercury

Name ______________________________ Date ________________

What Do You Remember?
Lesson 3 Review Questions

1. How long is a day on Mercury?

2. How long is a year on Mercury?

3. Describe the shape of Mercury's orbit.

4. Is it hot or cold on Mercury? Explain why.

5. Is Mercury a terrestrial planet or a gaseous planet?

6. What does the surface of Mercury look like and why?

7. How would the sky appear if you were on Mercury?

8. When is the best time to see Mercury and why?

Mercury

Mariner 10

How old was your mom when Mariner 10 first visited Mercury? If she was born after 1974, try to find out how old your grandma was.

"Every good gift and every perfect gift is from above, and comes down from the Father of lights." James 1:17

"Every good gift and every perfect gift is from above, and comes down from the Father of lights." James 1:17

Vocabulary Crossword

Lesson 3

MARINER 10

CRATER

GASEOUS

ASTEROIDS

TRANSIT

TERRESTRIAL

UNMANNED

					1							
	2											
								3				
			4									
		5										
6												
						7						

Across

2. The spacecraft that passed near Mercury in 1974 and 1975 **(put a space between the two words)**.
5. This word means to pass over. We use this word to describe when Mercury passes between the earth and the sun.
6. Planets that are “earth-like,” having a solid surface upon which you can stand.
7. Planets that are not solid, but instead are made of gas.

Down

1. A spacecraft that travels without a person inside.
3. Rocks that orbit in space, sometimes crashing into planets and other satellites.
4. A hole on the surface of a planet or moon caused by the impact of an asteroid.

My Mercury Project

What I did:

What I learned:

Mercury

TAKE IT FURTHER

LESSON 3

ALTERNATIVE IMPACT CRATER EXPERIMENT

In this experiment, you will take the book's crater activity even further. You will study how the impact crater's size is affected by the size of the object and the height from which it fell. You will only need 3 pebbles. You can also use balls, marbles, or any other small object – it does not have to be round.

In addition to the experiment items listed in the book (p. 37), you will need:

Dry powder paint
A flour sifter or sieve
A balance or postal scale for weighing the pebbles
A ruler
Tweezers or small kitchen tongs
An old newspaper to protect the work area

Put down some old newspaper or a table covering to catch any stray powder from the bowl. On top of the flour, use the flour sifter to sift a thin layer of colored powder paint. Now, find the weight and diameter of each of your pebbles (you can use other items like different sized balls or marbles if pebbles are not available). Record these numbers on a chart.

Take the smallest pebble, hold it one foot above the bowl and drop it into the bowl. Carefully, with tweezers or tongs, remove the pebble and measure the depth and width, as well as the average length of the rays that project out from the impact. The rays are white streaks of flour radiating from the crater. If it's easier for you, you can measure the depth by measuring the pebble and then measuring how far it protrudes from the surface. Subtracting that number from the pebble will give you the depth of the impact. Record all your data on the table below. Write down anything else you notice about the impact.

Now repeat the procedure with the same pebble, dropping it first two feet, then four feet and then, standing on a chair, from six feet above the bowl. Create a table like the one below for each height and record your measurements on the correct table after each impact.

Repeat the same procedure with all the pebbles, from biggest to smallest. When you are done, write down the total (adding all the numbers together) and then find the average by dividing the total by three. After you have studied your tables, make a conclusion about how big of an average impact you might have if an object fell from three feet, five feet and six feet. Test your hypothesis!

Record your data on the table below:

1 Foot	1st Object	2nd Object	3rd Object	Total	Average
Crater Width					
Crater Depth					
Ray Length					
Observations					

Fascinating Facts

Name ______________________________ Date ______________

What Do You Remember?
Lesson 4 Review Questions

1. Why did astronomers think Venus was a twin of the earth?

2. What would it feel like on Venus?

3. What is the atmosphere like on Venus?

4. What is special about the rotation of Venus?

5. How do we know what the surface of Venus looks like?

6. Why does Venus go through phases?

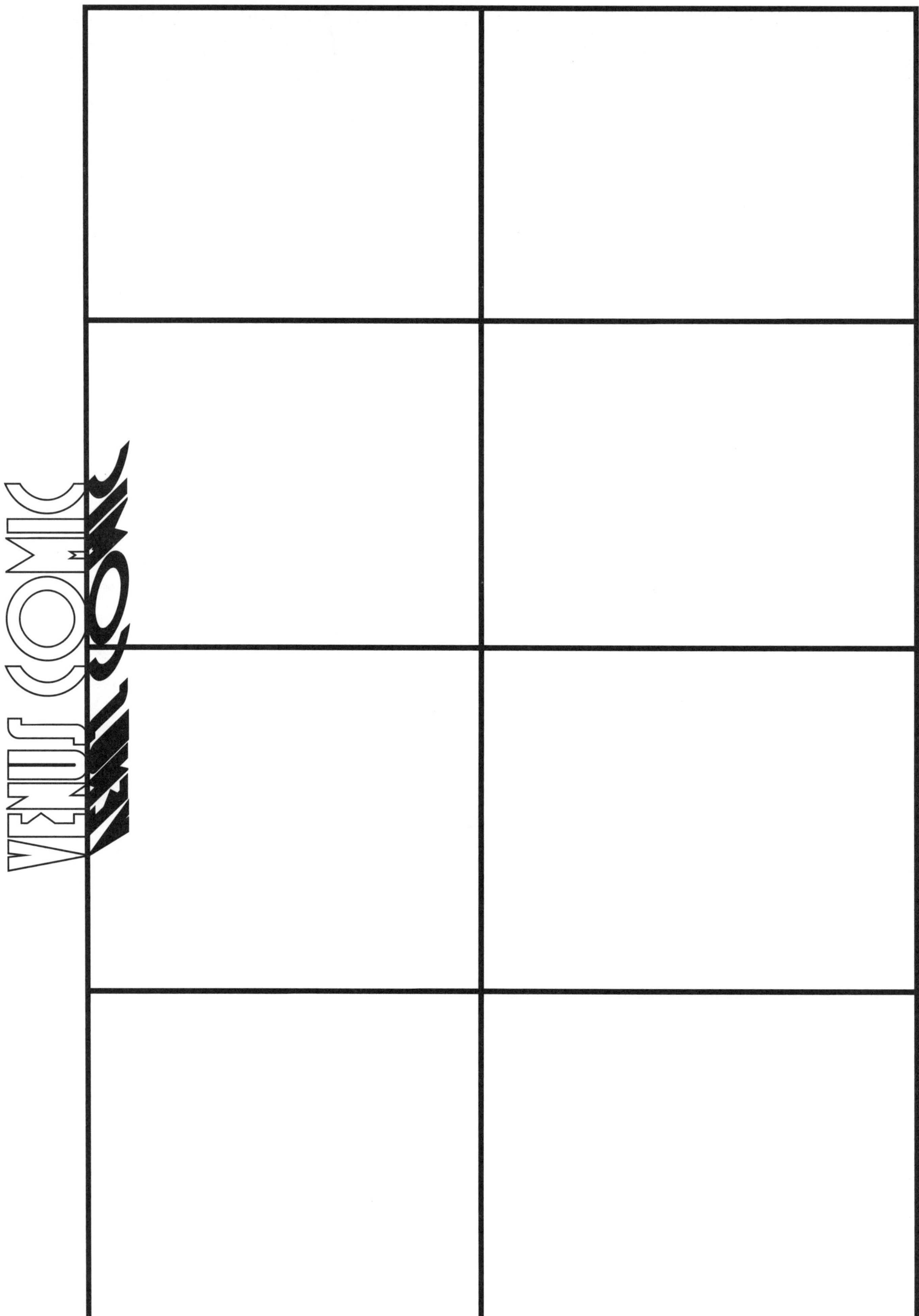
VENUS COMIC

And the light shines in darkness; and the darkness comprehended it not. John 1:5

And the light shines in darkness; and the darkness comprehended it not. John 1:5

Vocabulary Crossword

Lesson 4

EVENING STAR   RADAR   LAVA   CRESCENT   MORNING STAR   SULFURIC ACID

Across

1. The different shapes Venus appears to take as it orbits the sun.
3. A curved shape, like that of the moon when it is less than half illuminated.
5. Molten or melted rock that flows from a volcano.
6. A name given to Venus when it is visible in the early morning just before the sun rises **(put a space between the two words)**.
7. The toxic chemical in the heat-trapping clouds that cover Venus **(put a space between the two words)**.

Down

2. The name given to Venus when it is visible just after the sun sets in the sky **(put a space between the two words)**.
4. A device that sends out signals that bounce off the surface of an object and return to the device, revealing information about that object.

What I did:

What I learned:

RADAR CHART FOR VENUS EXPERIMENT

1	2	3	4	5	6	7	8	9	10
11	12	13	14	15	16	17	18	19	20
21	22	23	24	25	26	27	28	29	30
31	32	33	34	35	36	37	38	39	40
41	42	43	44	45	46	47	48	49	50
51	52	53	54	55	56	57	58	59	60
61	62	63	64	65	66	67	68	69	70
71	72	73	74	75	76	77	78	79	80

RADAR CHART FOR VENUS EXPERIMENT

1	2	3	4	5	6	7	8	9	10
11	12	13	14	15	16	17	18	19	20
21	22	23	24	25	26	27	28	29	30
31	32	33	34	35	36	37	38	39	40
41	42	43	44	45	46	47	48	49	50
51	52	53	54	55	56	57	58	59	60
61	62	63	64	65	66	67	68	69	70
71	72	73	74	75	76	77	78	79	80

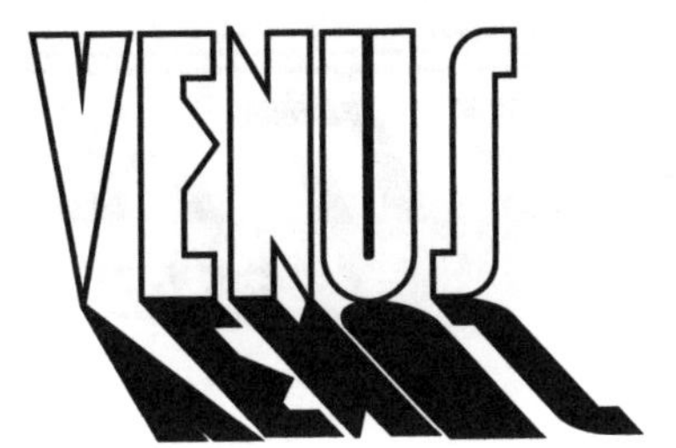
VENUS

TAKE IT FURTHER

LESSON 4

Alternate Venus Radar Ideas

Instead of using Plaster of Paris, you can build your Venus terrain using any of the following items:

Legos
Blocks
Toys and stuffed animals
Newspaper and duct tape

You will want to make certain that which ever objects you choose, they do not move around in the box. You might want to tape them to the bottom of the box.

Fascinating Facts

about Earth

FASCINATING FACTS

Name ______________________________ Date ____________

What Do You Remember?
Lesson 5 Review Questions

1. Name seven things that make Earth the only planet that can support life, and write a brief explanation about how each works to support life:

    1)

    2)

    3)

    4)

    5)

    6)

    7)

2. Why do we have different seasons?

3. What are the four major sections of the earth?

Earth

For by Him all things were created, both in the heavens and on earth...all things have been created by Him and for Him.

Colossians 1:16

For by Him all things were created, both in the heavens and on earth...all things have been created by Him and for Him.

Colossians 1:16

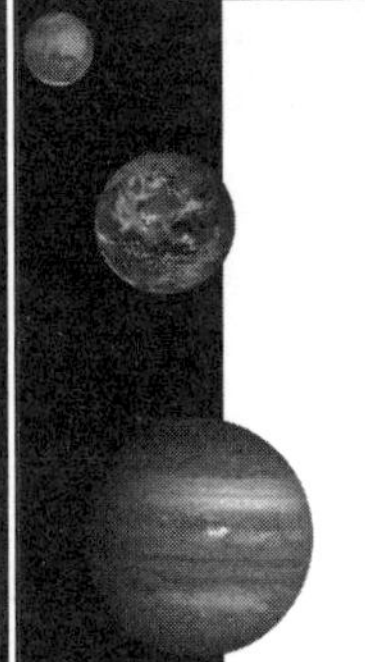

Vocabulary Crossword

Lesson 5

CRUST
MANTLE
INNER CORE
MASS
HEMISPHERE
EQUATOR
SHOOTING STAR
MAGNETOSPHERE
MATTER
OUTER CORE

Across

5. The imaginary line or circle around the center of the earth that divides the entire earth into two hemispheres.
6. The solid center of the earth **(put a space between the two words)**.
7. The property that indicates how much matter is contained in an object.
9. The section of the earth below the mantle and above the central inner core, made up of melted metals like nickel and iron **(put a space between the two words)**.
10. The layer of the earth just below the earth's crust and above the earth's core.

Down

1. Half of the earth. The top half is the Northern ____________. The bottom half is the Southern ____________.
2. The stuff that makes up everything around you. Anything that occupies space.
3. A rock from space that hits the earth's atmosphere and burns up **(put a space between the two words)**.
4. A large magnetic field that surrounds the earth and some other planets.
8. The solid outermost layer of the earth.

What I did:

What I learned:

LESSON 3

Extend your Earth Studies

Earth Books:

The Librarian Who Measured the Earth by Kathryn Lasky
Magic School Bus Inside the Earth by Joanna Cole
Journey to the Center of the Earth by Jules Verne (book, audio book, or movie)

Teach about Weather:

The Kid's Book of Weather Forecasting: Build a Weather Station, 'Read the Sky' & Make Predictions! (Williamson Kids Can! Series) by Mark Breen

Teach about Geology:

The Geology Book (Wonders of Creation) by John David Morris
Dry Bones and Other Fossils by Gary Parker
Geology Rocks! by Cindy Blobaum (may contain evolutionary content)

FASCINATING FACTS

Name ______________________________ Date ______________

What Do You Remember?
Lesson 6 Review Questions

1. What is the atmosphere like on the moon?

2. What is the color of the moon's sky during the moon's daytime?

3. Can you explain why the moon has phases?

4. What is a lunar eclipse?

5. Why are the astronaut's footprints probably still on the moon?

6. How does the moon affect the ocean?

7. How is this helpful to the earth?

The Moon

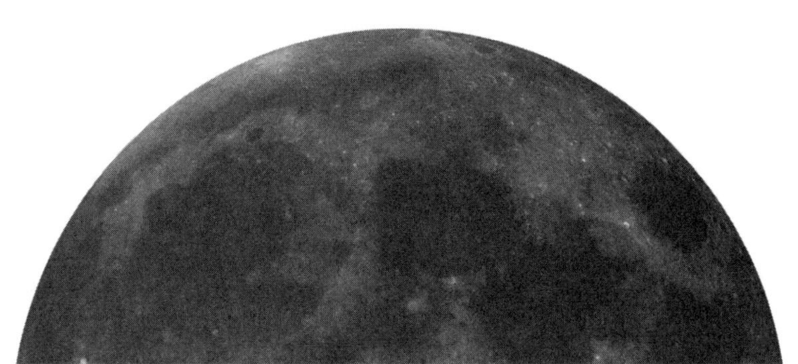

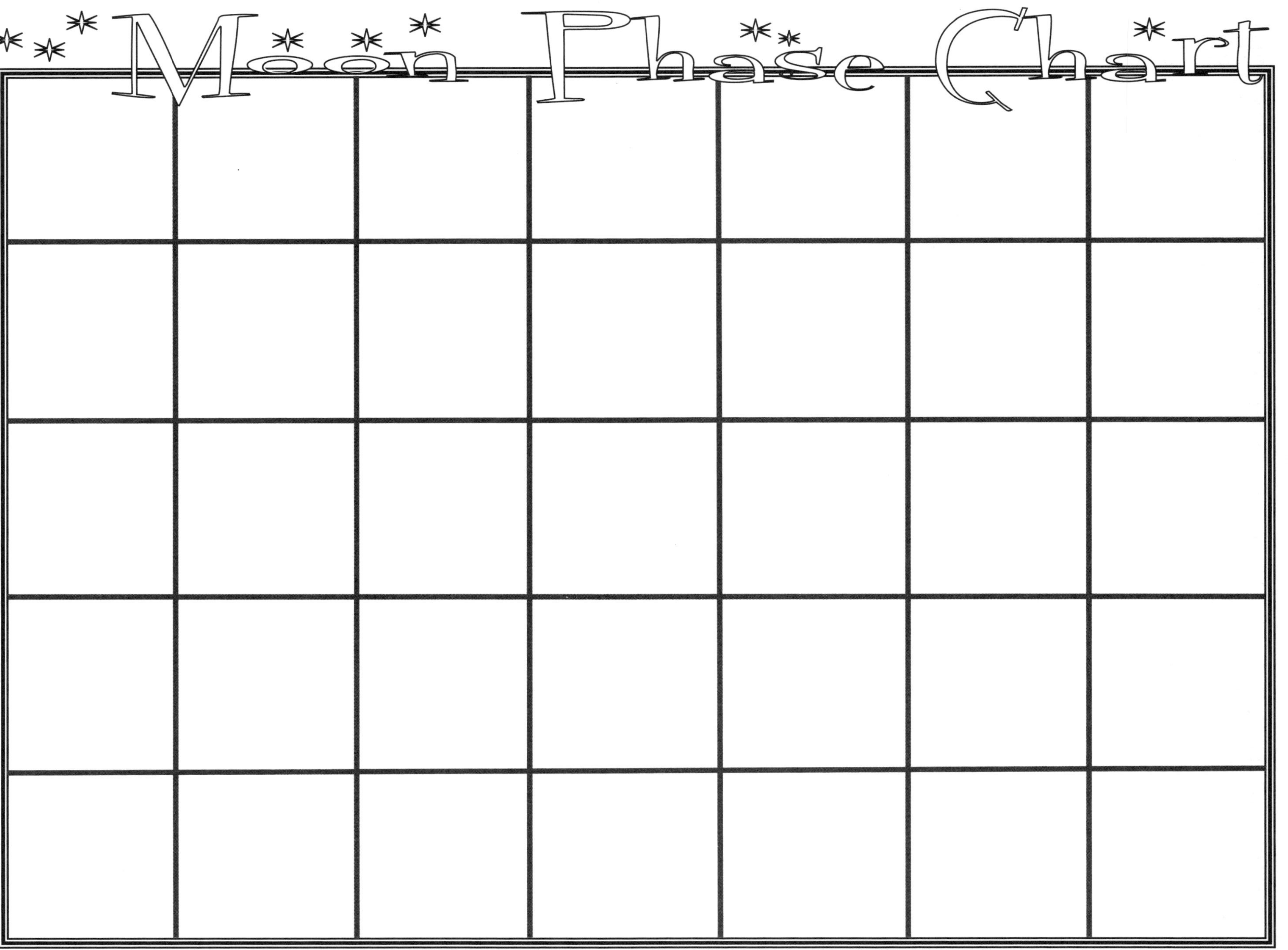
Moon Phase Chart

He made the moon for the seasons; the sun knows the place of its setting.

Psalm 104:19

He made the moon for the seasons; the sun knows the place of its setting.

Psalm 104:19

Vocabulary Crossword

Lesson 6

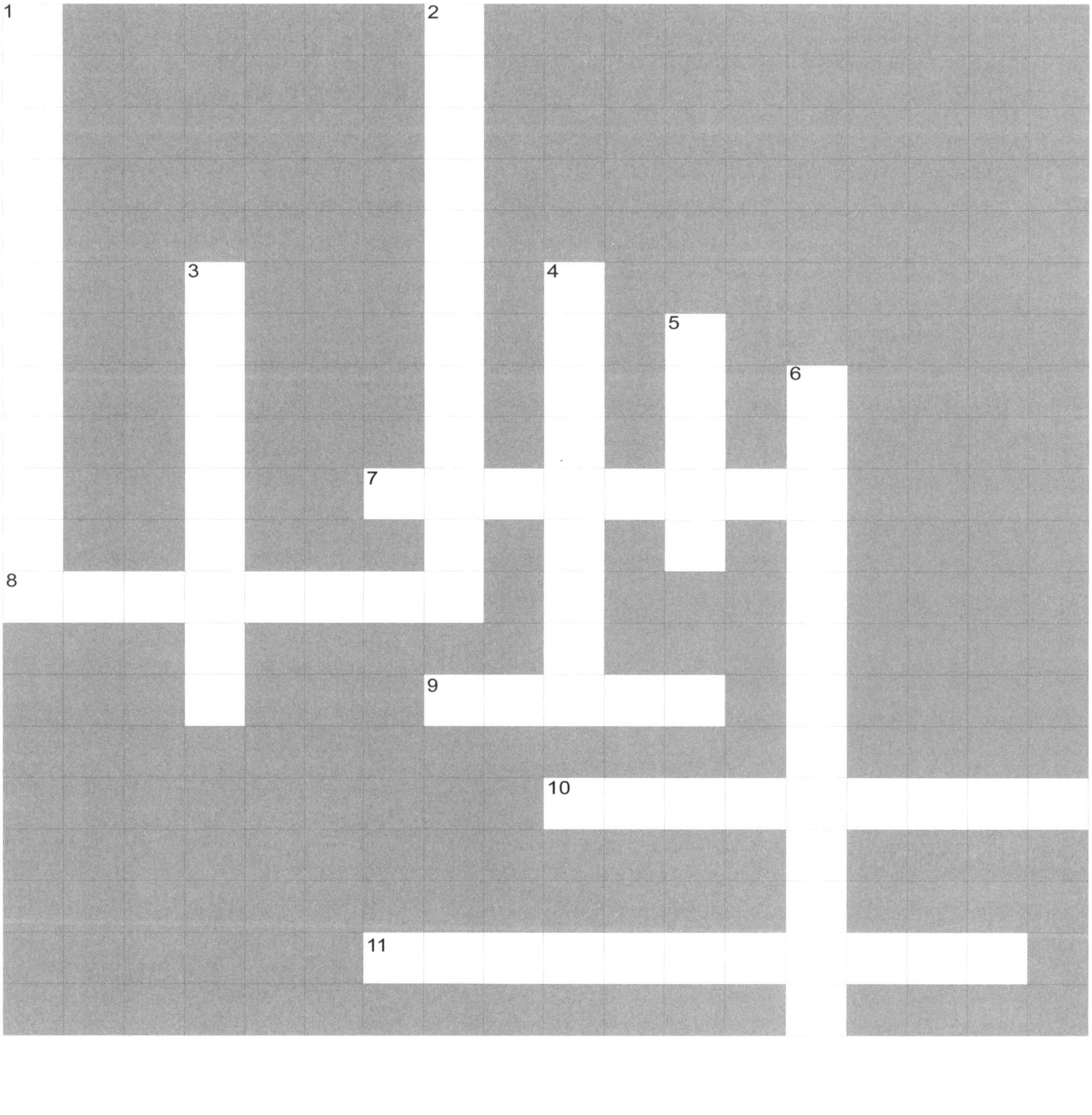

1 2 3 4 5 6 7 8 9 10 11

Vocabulary Crossword

Lesson 6

LOW TIDE	GIBBOUS MOON
NEW MOON	APOLLO 11
LUNAR	FULL MOON
HIGH TIDE	MARIA
LUNAR ROVER	CRESCENT MOON
QUARTER MOON	

Across

7. This is what we call it when the moon's gravity causes the water level of the ocean to be low at a particular place **(put a space between the two words)**.
8. This is what we call the moon when it is completely dark to the earth. This happens about once a month, at the beginning of the moon's cycle **(put a space between the two words)**.
9. A word used in reference to or relating to the moon.
10. What we call it when the ocean bulges towards the moon and floods over the land, causing the water to be at its highest level at a particular place **(put a space between the two words)**.
11. A kind of vehicle used to explore the moon **(put a space between the two words)**.

Down

1. This is what we call the moon when we can see exactly half of the moon lit up, making a half circle **(put a space between the two words)**.
2. This is what we call the moon when it is more than half illuminated. It occurs right before a full moon **(put a space between the two words)**.
3. The first spacecraft to land on the moon **(put a space between the two words)**.
4. How the moon looks to the earth when the entire moon is visible and lit up **(put a space between the two words)**.
5. Dark patches on the surface of the moon that are smooth, flat plains. The side of the moon that always faces the earth has a lot of these patches.
6. This is what we call the moon immediately after the new moon, until the first quarter **(put a space between the two words)**.

My Moon Project

What I did:

What I learned:

The Moon

TAKE IT FURTHER

LESSON 6

Draw the Moon

Go outside with a pair of binoculars. To still the binoculars, set them on a tripod or steady them on the back of a solid surface, such as a chair. Center the binoculars on the moon and draw the moon with crayons as you see it through the binoculars. You can glue your drawing onto the Moon Project Page.

Make Moon Cookies

To further the activity above, you can bake large round cookies and attempt to recreate the moon's surface with icing.

Earth and Moon to Scale Activity

* This activity is a guessing game designed for your parent to do with you. Have your parent follow the instructions below.

You will need:
Different sized balls - One should be 1/4th the size of the others (read the full instructions before gathering the balls).

Have your children guess which two balls accurately represent the size of the earth to the moon. After they have made their guess, tell them that four moons laid side by side equal the diameter of the earth (be sure you have two balls that can accurately represent the earth and the moon). Now, have them search for the two balls that would be a scale model of the earth and moon.

Next, with the two balls, have your students guess how far away the moon is from the earth. Separate the two balls to that distance, reminding your students what it means to be "to scale" and how the size is reduced based on the size of the balls.

The actual distance between the earth and moon would be close to putting 30 earths side by side, or 110 moons side by side. Show your students the actual size and distance difference between the earth and moon.

Moon Jumps

On the moon, because the gravity is weaker than the earth's gravity, you could jump six times as high as you can on the earth.

Let's find out exactly how high you could jump on the moon! You will need masking tape and a yard stick or measuring tape. With a piece of masking tape in your hand, jump up as high as you can next to a wall and stick the masking tape on the wall at that height. Measure how high you were able to jump (or how high you were able to reach in your jump). Then take that number and multiply it by six. That's how high you could jump on the moon.

FASCINATING FACTS

ABOUT

MARS

Name ______________________________ Date ______________

What Do You Remember?
Lesson 7 Review Questions

1. What makes Mars look red?

2. What is the atmosphere like on Mars?

3. What is the surface like on Mars?

4. What is the name of the biggest volcano in our solar system?

5. Tell about the moons of Mars.

6. How long does it take Mars to revolve and rotate?

7. What is the weather like on Mars?

8. Why do astronomers think Mars would be a good place to visit and perhaps live?

S MARS MARS MARS MARS MARS MARS MARS MARS M

Oh LORD, our Lord, how majestic is Your name in all the earth, Who have displayed Your splendor above the heavens!

Psalm 8:1

Oh LORD, our Lord, how majestic is Your name in all the earth, Who have displayed Your splendor above the heavens!

Psalm 8:1

Vocabulary Crossword

Lesson 7

OLYMPUS MONS
ECOSYSTEM
PHOBOS
POLAR ICECAPS
DRY ICE
PERMAFROST
DEIMOS

Across

3. The largest moon orbiting Mars.
5. Frozen carbon dioxide **(put a space between the two words)**.
6. Ground water that is considered permanently frozen.
7. The smaller moon orbiting Mars.

Down

1. A special habitat that can sustain life. On Mars, an artificial __________ would be an enclosed structure sealing in oxygen, allowing the sun's light to penetrate, containing all that is needed to sustain life on Mars.
2. Large slabs of ice at the North and South Poles of the planet Mars **(put a space between the two words)**.
4. The largest volcano in our solar system **(put a space between the two words).**

MY MARS PROJECT

What I did:

What I learned:

MARS

TAKE IT FURTHER

LESSON 7

Why is the Red Planet Red? Experiment

Scientists think Mars was once flowing with water and lava bursting from active volcanoes. They believe the red color of the planet was produced by rusting iron. This iron could only rust in a wet environment. In this activity, you will come to understand how a planet that had a great deal of iron could become red.

You will need:
Two pie pans
Light-colored sand
Steel wool
Scissors
A magnifying glass
Water

Fill both pie pans with sand. Cut the steel wool into tiny pieces and mix it with the sand. Pour water into one pie pan until it is very wet, but not flooded. Keep the other pie pan completely dry. The wet pie pan is your variable pan. The dry pie pan is your constant pan. Study both pans with the magnifying glass. Make a guess about what will happen at the end of the week. Make certain the variable pie pan remains damp all week. Each day, check on the pie pans and observe the differences. Study with a magnifying glass at the end of the week to observe both pans. If you'd like, you can continue this experiment until the end of the month.

Make an Edible Mars Rover

Using pictures found on the Internet, recreate a Mars Rover (such as Sojourner or Pathfinder) using tasty treats.

You will need:
Icing to put the rover together
Graham crackers
Round cookies for the wheels
Twizzlers and other assorted candy to make different components

Take a picture before you eat it! Be sure to glue your picture onto the Mars Project Page.

Sojourner

FASCINATING FACTS

ABOUT

Space Rocks

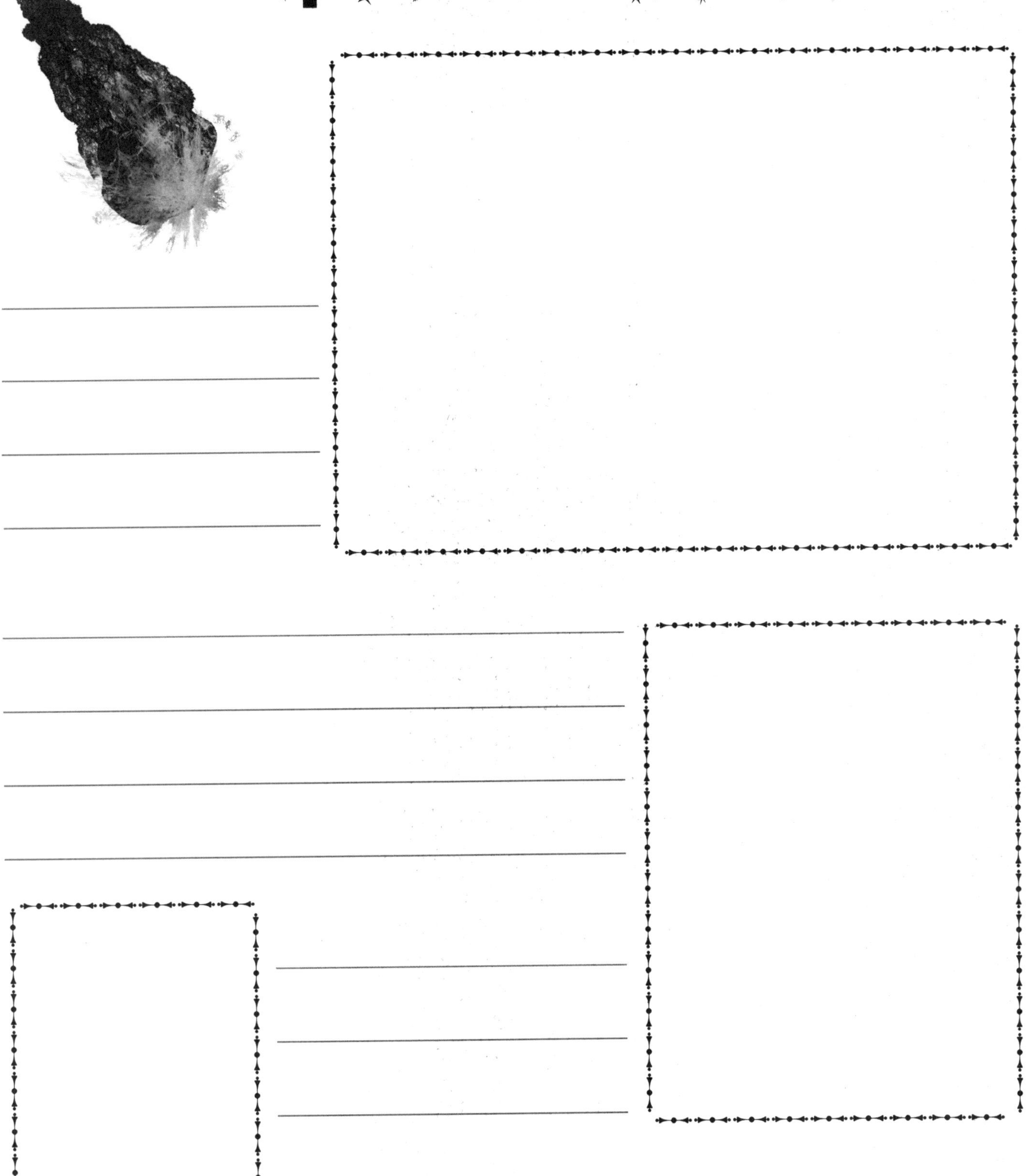

Name ______________________________ Date______________

What Do You Remember?
Lesson 8 Review Questions

1. What is another name for a comet?

2. What does a comet leave behind as it orbits the sun?

3. What happens when a comet's dust particles enter our atmosphere?

4. What do people call meteors?

5. What is a meteor called when it hits the earth?

6. Where have many meteorites been found?

7. From which planet did some of the meteorites come?

8. Where is the asteroid belt located?

9. What is the Exploded Planet Hypothesis?

10. Can you give some reasons why this might be a correct hypothesis?

Comets

"head of hair" a star with hair

large rock + ice that orbit around our sun

Meteors

smaller rocks that burn up in our atmosphere

Asteroids

large rocks that orbit our sun

Meteor Showers

Shower Name	Approximate date to see	Name of comet	Number of shooting stars per hour
Quadrantids	January 3	Unknown	40
Pi Puppids	April 5	Unknown	40
Lyrids	April 22	Comet Thatcher	15
Eta Aquarids	May 5	Comet Halley	20
Delta Aquarids	July 30	Unknown	20
Perseids*	August 12	Comet Swift-Tuttle	50
Orionids	October 22	Comet Halley	25
Taurids	November 4	Comet Encke	15
Leonids	November 17	Comet Temple-Tuttle	15
Geminids*	December 14	Asteroid 3200 Phaethon	50
Ursids	December 23	Comet Tuttle	20

* Indicates large meteor showers

Trust in the LORD forever, for in GOD the LORD, we have an everlasting Rock.

Isaiah 26:4

Trust in the LORD forever, for in GOD the LORD, we have an everlasting Rock.

Isaiah 26:4

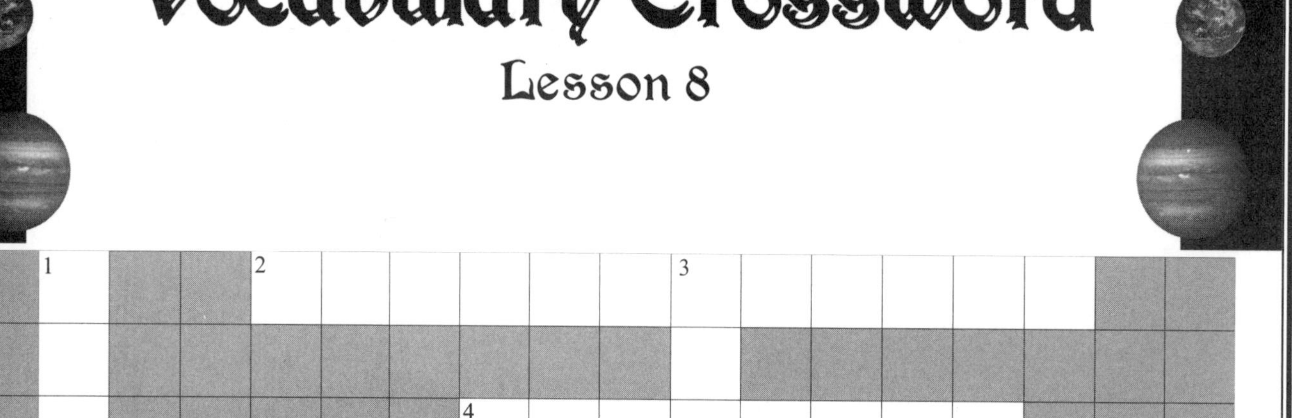

Vocabulary Crossword

Lesson 8

Vocabulary Crossword

Lesson 8

METEOR SHOWER
LONG-PERIOD
PERSEID
COMA
SHORT-PERIOD
STARDUST
NUCLEUS
HALLEY
INNER PLANETS
ASTEROID BELT
METEOROIDS
OUTER PLANETS
COMET
METEORITES
ASTEROIDS

Across

2. A comet that orbits the sun every 200 years or less is called a ___________ comet **(put a dash between the two words)**.
4. The first NASA spacecraft designed to study a comet.
7. Dirt and small rocks or pebbles floating in space that become meteors when they enter the earth's atmosphere.
10. A comet that orbits the sun every 201 years or more is called a _____________comet **(put a dash between the two words)**.
11. A large ball of ice mixed with rocks and dirt, having a long luminous tail when its orbit passes close to the sun.
12. A particular comet that occurs every 76 years, named after the man who discovered it by studying ancient records.
13. Meteors that have entered the earth's atmosphere and fallen to the ground without completely burning up.
14. Large rocks orbiting the sun in space (ranging in size from several feet long to larger than a football field).
15. The space between Mars and Jupiter where millions of asteroids orbit the sun **(put a space between the two words)**.

Down

1. A _________ occurs when the earth crosses the orbit of a comet, causing the leftover dust and debris to enter our atmosphere, resulting in a large number of shooting stars **(put a space between the two words)**.
3. The meteor shower that occurs every August.
5. A ball of steam and dust coming from and surrounding a comet.
6. The _______ are all the gaseous planets located outside the asteroid belt **(put a space between the two words)**.
8. These are the planets that are found between the sun and the asteroid belt **(put a space between the two words)**.
9. The center of a comet, made up of ice and a large rock in the interior.

My Space Rocks Project

What I did:

What I learned:

Space Rocks

TAKE IT FURTHER

LESSON 8

Solar System Model Options

Here are two optional activities to help you understand the distance between the planets. In both activities, you will need something to represent each planet and the sun. You can use the objects from the lesson on page 101, or something that is not to scale, such as marshmallows. In both activities, you will need a long hallway—such as you might find in a church.

Planet	# of Sheets or Paper Clips from sun	# of Sheets or Paper Clips from previous planet
Mercury	4	4
Venus	7	3
Earth	10	3
Mars	15	5
Jupiter	52	37
Saturn	96	44
Uranus	192	96
Neptune	300	108

Toilet Paper Model or Paper Clip Model

Using a roll of toilet paper or 392 paper clips, each sheet or clip represents 10,000,000 miles. Begin placing toilet paper sheets or paper clips from the sun to each planet in our solar system.

Dry Ice Comet Model

If you are feeling very adventurous, this activity is great fun for classes, giving everyone a real feel for comets. You can find dry ice in the yellow pages by searching under "ice." Make sure to bring an ice chest to transport the dry ice from the place of purchase to your freezer. ***Remember that dry ice can be a dangerous chemical, so please use caution and only do this activity with adult supervision.***

You will need:
2 cups of water
2 cups of dry ice (frozen carbon dioxide)
2 spoonfuls of sand or dirt
A dash of ammonia
A large plastic mixing bowl
4 plastic garbage bags (put three of them inside of each other to make 1 three-ply bag)
Work gloves
A hammer
A large mixing spoon

Directions:
Line your mixing bowl with a garbage bag.
Pour in 2 cups of water.
Add sand or dirt and stir.
Add ammonia.
Add corn syrup and stir.
Put on your gloves.
Place the dry ice in the three-ply bag.
Pound and crush the dry ice using the hammer.
Add the dry ice to the mixing bowl, while stirring.
Stir until the mixture is frozen.
Use the bag in the bowl to shape the materials into a ball.
Unwrap the ball once it is frozen. This is your comet.

Model of Solar System with Asteroid Belt

On a sheet of construction paper, draw our solar system with colored markers, leaving a space for the asteroid belt. After drawing all the planets, use glue to trace the path of the asteroid belt. Sprinkle sand, salt, pepper, or glitter over the page so that it sticks to the glue, simulating the asteroid belt.

Cartoon of Exploded Planet

Create a cartoon of the events that led up to and culminated in the alleged explosion of the planet between Mars and Jupiter.

FASCINATING FACTS ABOUT JUPITER

Fascinating Facts
about
Jupiter

Name ______________________________ Date ____________________

What Do You Remember?
Lesson 9 Review Questions

1. How does Jupiter protect the earth?

2. Why is Jupiter a little like the sun?

3. Explain what you know about the Great Red Spot.

4. Why does Jupiter have stripes?

5. Name Jupiter's largest moons.

6. Why are they called Galilean moons?

7. Describe Amalthea.

8. Tell about the spacecraft Galileo.

For You light my lamp; the LORD my God illumines my darkness. Psalm 18:28

For You light my lamp;
the LORD my God
illumines my darkness.
Psalm 18:28

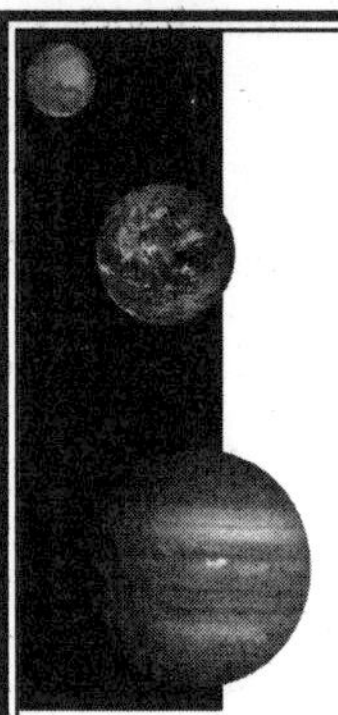

Vocabulary Crossword

Lesson 9

1 2 3 4 5 6 7 8 9

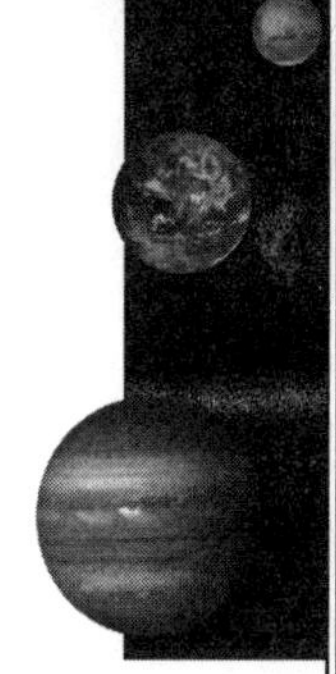

Vocabulary Crossword

Lesson 9

HYDROGEN

GREAT RED SPOT

GANYMEDE

CALLISTO

JOVIAN

GALILEAN MOONS

EUROPA

GAS GIANT

IO

HELIUM

Across

3. Jupiter's biggest moon. This moon is larger than the planet Mercury. It's made of ice and rocks and is covered with craters.
4. The word used when referring to Jupiter.
6. The smallest Galilean moon, believed to be covered with a large, frozen ocean. It is the smoothest object in the entire solar system.
7. The name given to a planet in the outer solar system because it is made of gases and is very large **(leave a space between the two words)**.
8. A gas found on the planet Jupiter. It is also found in balloons that float.
9. The second smallest of the four Galilean moons, also the most colorful. It contains hot, active volcanoes filled with sulfur (that might make the planet smell like rotten eggs).

Down

1. The name given to the giant storm on Jupiter **(leave spaces between the three words)**.
2. The _____________ refer to Jupiter's four largest moons, discovered by Galileo **(leave a space between the two words)**.
5. The Galilean moon that has no core but is simply a big ball of ice with rocks and boulders scattered throughout. It's much like a comet. It also has one of the largest impact craters in our solar system.
8. A main gas found on Jupiter besides helium.

My Jupiter Project

What I did:

What I learned:

JUPITER

TAKE IT FURTHER

LESSON 9

Planet Size Activity

It's been said that all the planets could fit inside Jupiter. You could do this experiment to see if that is true. You will need salt dough (or clay), a metric ruler, and the chart below to create a small scale model of each planet.

You can make your own salt dough using the recipe below.

Ingredients:
4 cups flour
1 cup salt
1-1/2 cups hot water
2 teaspoons vegetable oil

Mix the salt and flour together. While stirring, gradually add the water until the dough becomes elastic. Mix in the oil. If your dough is sticky, slowly add more flour. If it turns out too crumbly, add more water. Knead the dough until it's a nice consistency.

The numbers in the chart below compare the size of the planets to earth. Create the planets by forming balls. Measure each planet's diameter in centimeters by placing them against a ruler to make sure each one is the correct size. For example, Earth is 1.0 centimeters, and Mercury would be .38 centimeters or 3.8 millimeters.

Mercury	Venus	Earth	Mars	Jupiter	Saturn	Uranus	Neptune	Pluto
0.38	0.95	1.0	0.53	11.21	9.46	4.01	3.88	0.18

After you have created each one, take all the planets, except Jupiter, and roll them together to see how big of a planet they make. Are the combined planets bigger or smaller than Jupiter? Could they fit inside Jupiter?

FASCINATING FACTS

ABOUT

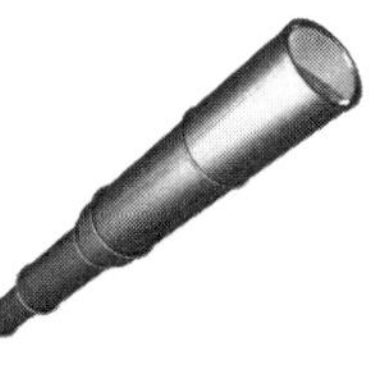

FASCINATING FACTS

ABOUT

Name ______________________________ Date ______________

What Do You Remember?
Lesson 10 Review Questions

1. What is Saturn made of?

2. Why would Saturn be an unpleasant place to visit?

3. Which planet is considered Saturn's twin?

4. What are Saturn's rings made of?

5. What do shepherd moons do?

6. How many years does it take Saturn to orbit the sun?

7. Why does Saturn look as if it is being squeezed?

8. What is the name of the space mission that went to Saturn?

SATURN

VENN DIAGRAM
JUPITER
SATURN

He counts the number of the stars; He gives names to all of them. Psalm 147:4

He counts the number of the stars; He gives names to all of them. Psalm 147:4

Vocabulary Crossword

Lesson 10

HUYGENS
SHEPHERD MOONS
TITAN
PROMETHEUS
PANDORA
CASSINI

Across

3. One of Saturn's shepherd moons.
4. Saturn's largest moon. It is close to the size of Mercury.
5. What we call Saturn's special moons that keep the rings on Saturn from spreading out too far **(leave a space between the two words)**.
6. The name of the man that discovered that Saturn's handles were actually rings around the planet. It's also the name of the probe that will collect and test samples of dirt from Titan, Saturn's moon.

Down

1. The name of the mission and the spacecraft that traveled to Saturn.
2. One of Saturn's shepherd moons.

What I did:

What I learned:

SATURN

TAKE IT FURTHER

LESSON 10

Make a Model of Saturn

You can make a beautiful model of Saturn that hangs from the ceiling.

You will need:

A yellow marker
A 2-3 inch Styrofoam ball
An unwanted CD
Glue
A paper clip
String
A tack
Glitter (gold and silver preferred)

Directions:

Begin by coloring the Styrofoam ball yellow with the marker. Cut the Styrofoam ball in half. Put glue on the flat insides of both halves. Place the CD inside these halves and put the ball back together with the CD in the center, resembling Saturn's rings.

Glue the glitter on the ball in stripes to create the colors of Saturn.

Insert the paper clip in the top of the ball. Attach string to the paper clip and hang the ball from the ceiling by tacking the other end of the string to the ceiling.

FASCINATING FACTS
ABOUT
Uranus and Neptune

FASCINATING FACTS

ABOUT

Uranus and Neptune

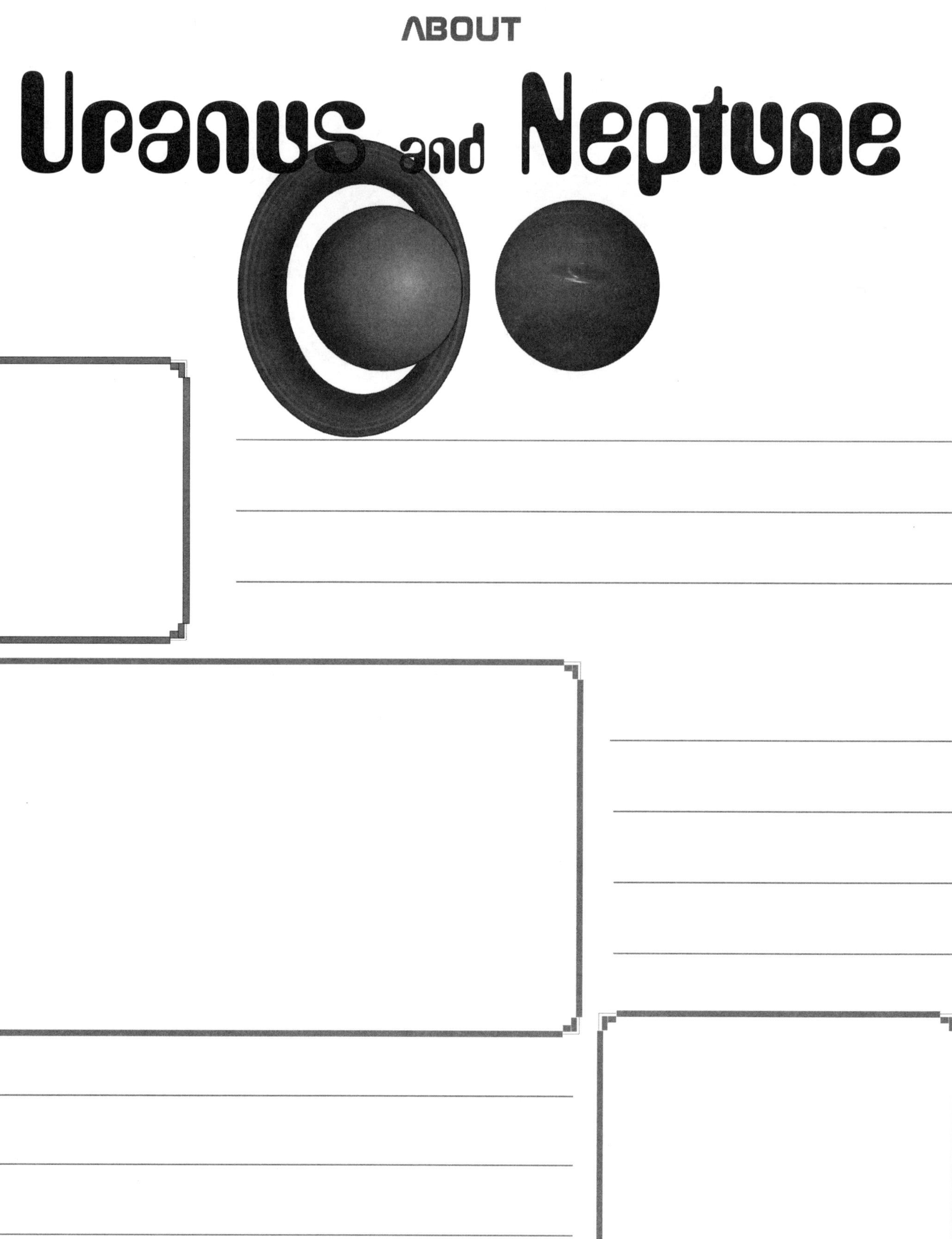

Name ____ Date ________________

What Do You Remember?
Lesson 11 Review Questions– Uranus

1. What chemical makes Uranus blue-green in appearance?

2. Why does Uranus look like a ball rolling around the sun?

3. What makes it look like a loose wagon wheel?

4. Why was it so exciting to discover Uranus?

5. Who discovered Uranus?

6. How were they educated?

7. How long does it take Uranus to orbit the sun?

Name ______________________________ Date ______________

What Do You Remember?

Lesson 11 Review Questions– Neptune

1. Why was Neptune discovered?

2. What made astronomers think there was another planet beyond Neptune?

3. What chemical gives Neptune its blue color?

4. Is Neptune the eighth planet from the sun?

5. How long does it take Neptune to revolve around the sun?

6. What was the Great Dark Spot?

7. What is the name of Neptune's biggest moon?

8. What are geysers?

9. Explain what you know about the geysers on Triton.

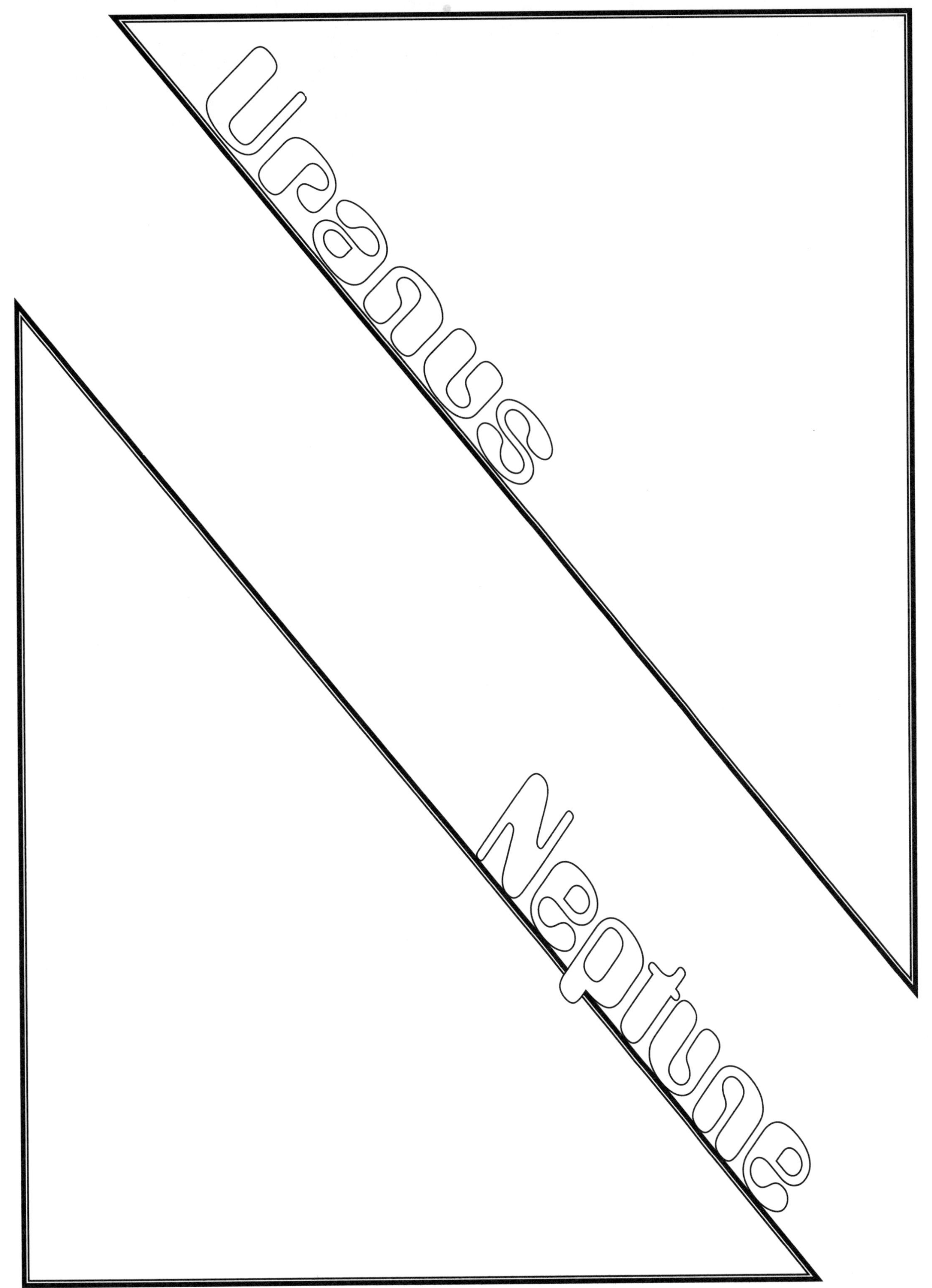
Uranus
Neptune

For as the heavens are higher than the
earth, so are My ways higher than your
ways, and My thoughts than your thoughts.

Isaiah 55:9

For as the heavens are higher
than the earth, so are My
ways higher than your ways,
and My thoughts than your
thoughts.

Isaiah 55:9

Vocabulary Crossword

Lesson 11

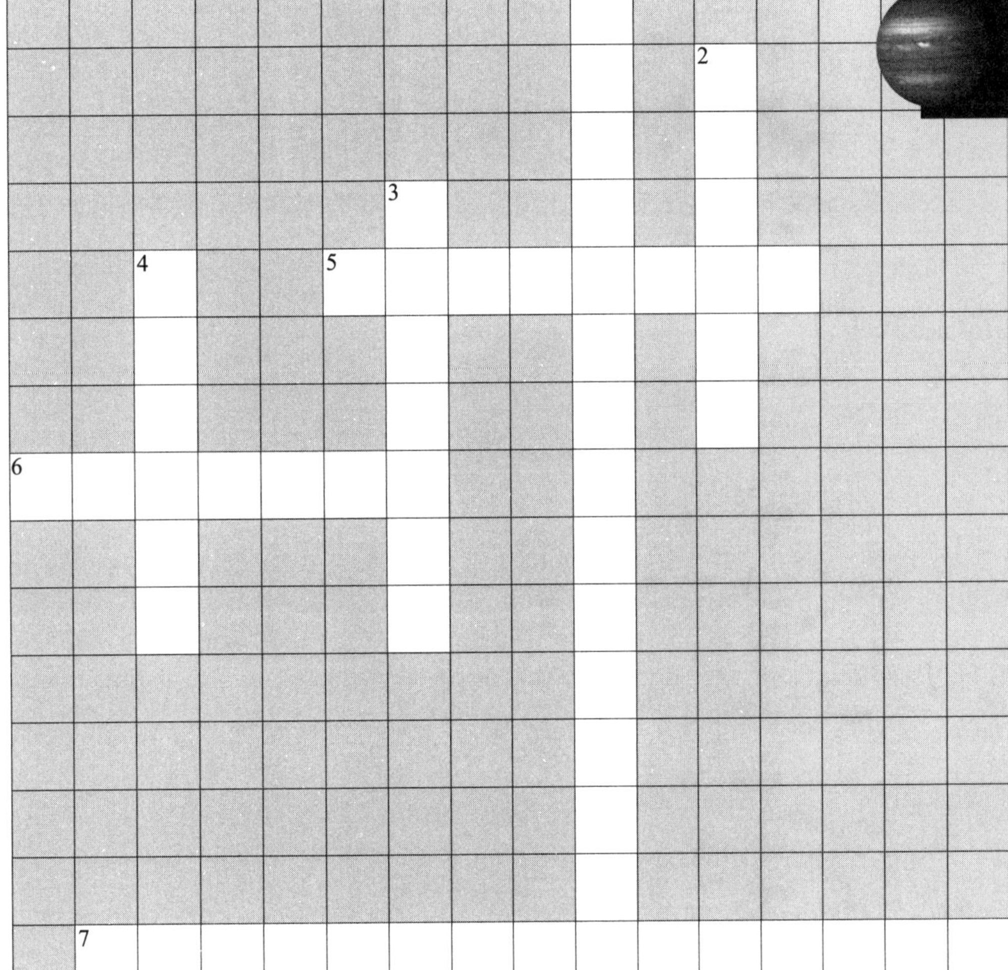

GREAT DARK SPOT
HERSCHEL
GEYSERS
TRITON
METHANE
EUREKA
HERSCHEL CRATER

Across

5. The last name of the two home educated children that discovered Uranus.
6. The gas that makes Uranus and Neptune appear blue.
7. A huge storm that was once visible on Neptune, but is not visible today **(put spaces between the three words)**.

Down

1. A huge crater on Saturn's moon, Mimas, that was named after the man who discovered both Uranus and Mimas **(put a space between the two words)**.
2. A word meaning, "I found it!"
3. Holes in the ground that spew hot water from underground springs.
4. The biggest of Neptune's moons.

My Uranus and Neptune Project

What I did:

What I learned:

Uranus and Neptune

TAKE IT FURTHER

LESSON 11

Satellite Graph

You can create a Satellite Graph and record the number of satellites each planet has. Simply create a graph, then chart each planet and their satellites. This will help you to visually demonstrate the difference in the number of satellites, as well as reinforce what you have learned.

Planet Mystery Questions

Now that you have learned about all the planets, create a mystery question game to be played with your siblings or friends. Each one think up different mystery planet clues—for example, "I have rust," or "I'm made of methane and have rings." Put the questions on index cards and play a game to see how many each of you can get correct.

Fascinating Facts

About

Pluto and the Kuiper Belt

FASCINATING FACTS

ABOUT

Pluto and the Kuiper Belt

Name ______________________________ Date ______________

What Do You Remember?
Lesson 12 Review Questions

1. What is the Kuiper belt?

2. How was Pluto discovered?

3. What are some of the strange features of Pluto?

4. Why do some astronomers believe Pluto is not a planet?

5. What do these astronomers think Pluto is?

6. What do you believe about the Pluto debate and why?

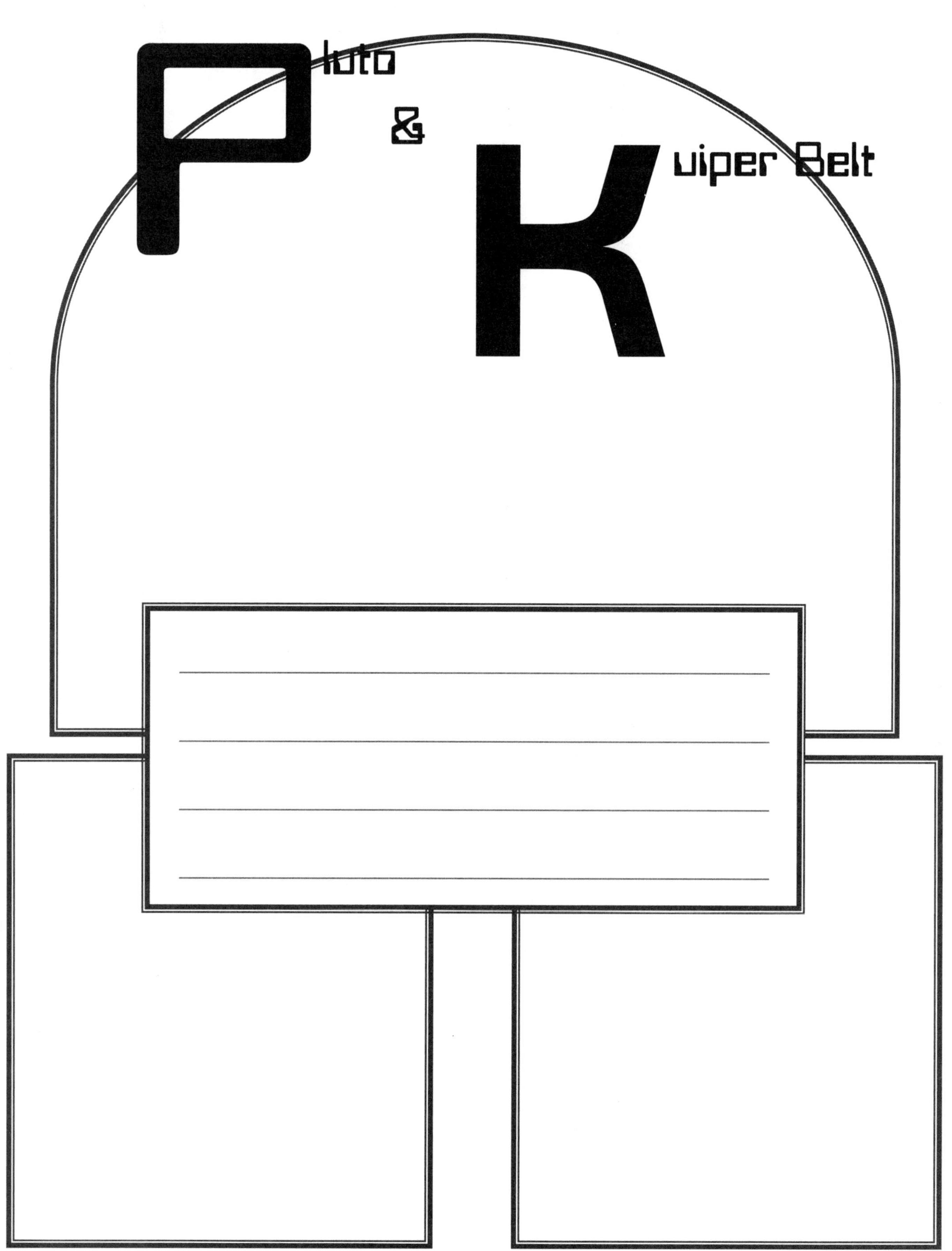
Pluto
&
Kuiper Belt

PLUTO DEBATE

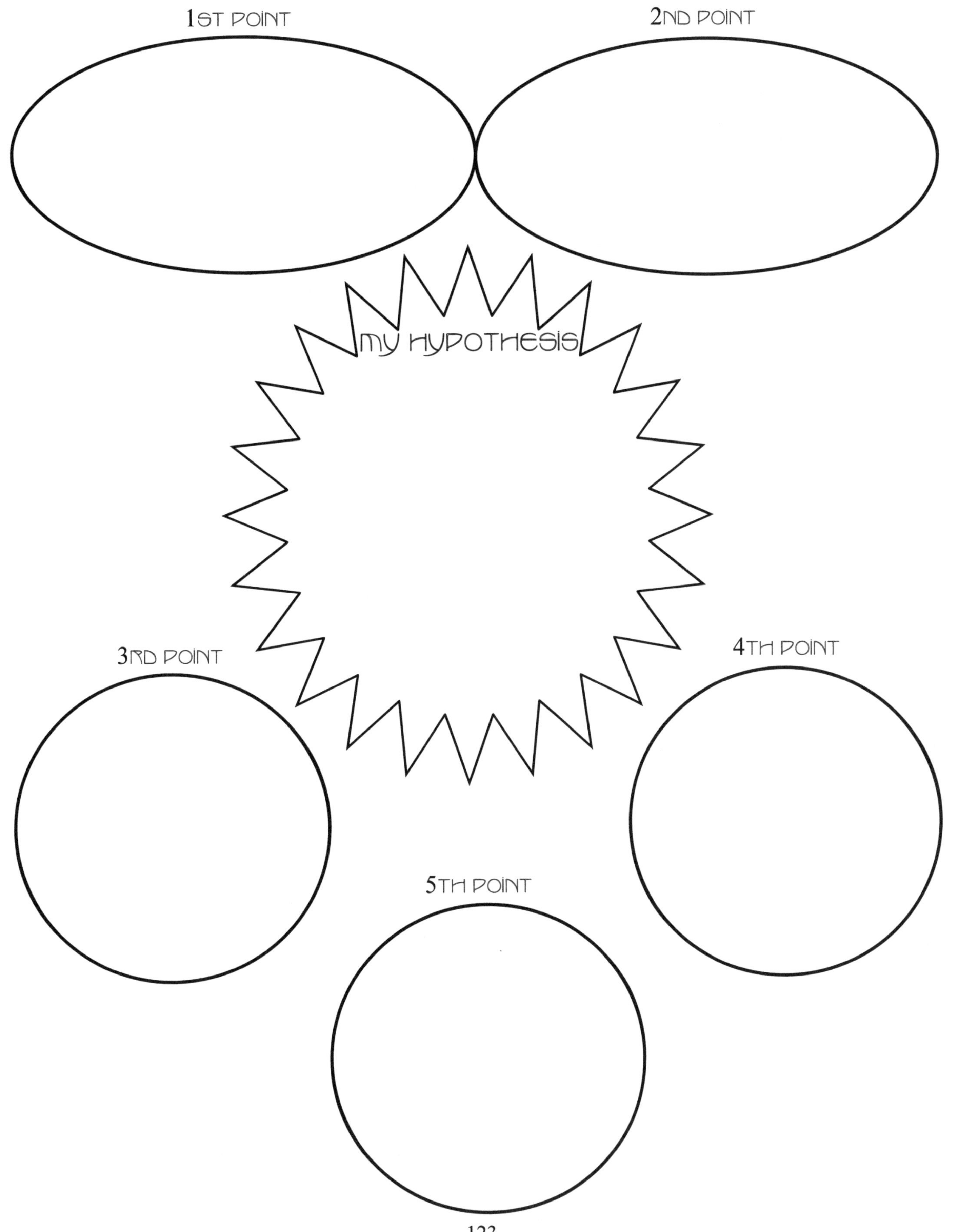

"Those who have insight will shine brightly like the brightness of the expanse of heaven, and those who lead the many to righteousness, like the stars forever and ever."

Daniel 12:3

"Those who have insight will shine brightly like the brightness of the expanse of heaven, and those who lead the many to righteousness, like the stars forever and ever."

Daniel 12:3

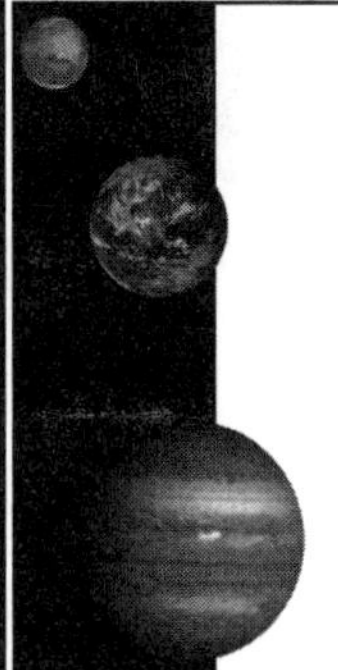

Vocabulary Crossword

Lesson 12

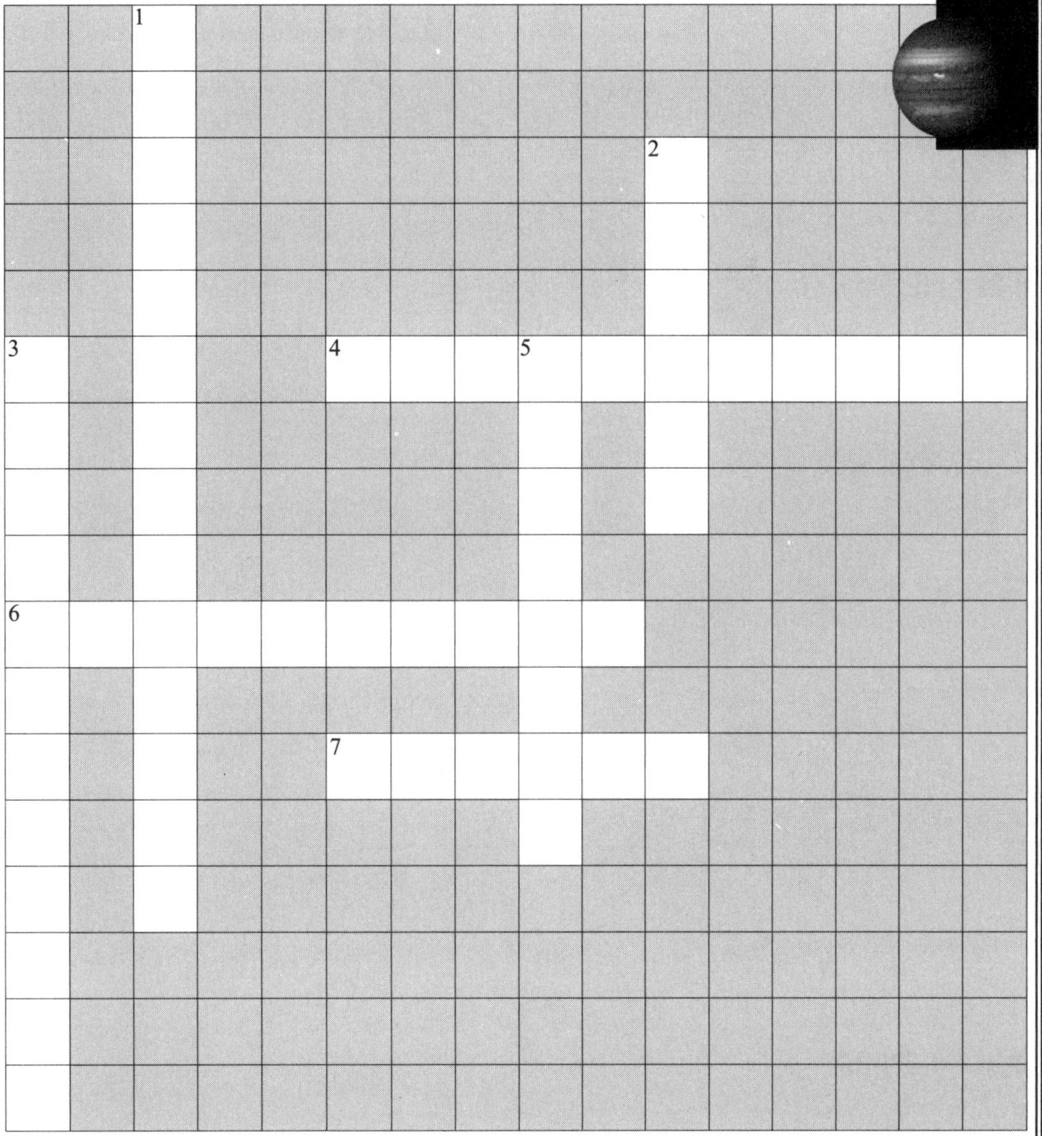

NEW HORIZONS
HYPOTHESIS
FREEZING POINT
KUIPER BELT
CHARON
QUAOAR
PLUTINOS

Across

4. A ring of comets and asteroids that orbit the sun outside our solar system **(put a space between the two words).**
6. A good guess based on the facts.
7. An object in the Kuiper belt that is about half the size of Pluto, discovered in 2002.

Down

1. The temperature at which a liquid freezes **(put a space between the two words)**.
2. The name of Pluto's moon.
3. The unmanned space craft that will reach Pluto in 2015 **(put a space between the two words)**.
5. Objects in the Kuiper belt that have the appearance of Pluto.

My Pluto & Kuiper Belt Project

What I did:

What I learned:

Pluto & the Kuiper Belt

TAKE IT FURTHER

LESSON 12

Pluto in History

It takes Pluto 248 years to orbit the earth. The last time Pluto was in the position it is in today, what was going on with the earth? Research what was happening on the earth 248 years ago. You can create a paper or poster of all the things that were going on. Include what people wore, where they lived, and how they ate. If you have any information about your personal ancestors, this might be a great time to discover what their lives were like 248 years ago.

Make a Construction Paper Model of the Solar System

Using the image found on page 132 of *Exploring Creation with Astronomy* as a guide, make a model of the solar system with Pluto and the Kuiper belt represented.

Create your model on construction paper, using yarn or string to represent the orbital path of the planets, Pluto, and the Kuiper belt. You might use beans or beads to represent each planet. Salt rocks or glitter might be a good thing to represent the Kuiper belt. Don't forget the asteroid belt in your model.

Fascinating Facts
about
Stars & Galaxies

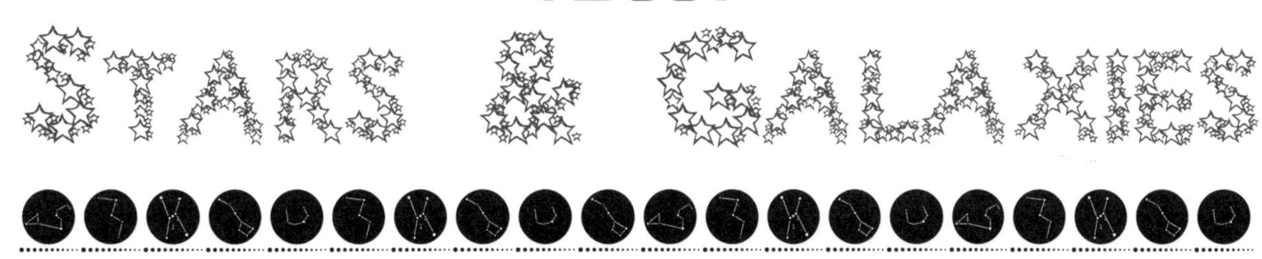

Star Temperature Mnemonic

O	B	A	F	G	K	M

Fascinating Facts
about
Stars & Galaxies

Name ____ Date __________________

What Do You Remember?
Lesson 13 Review Questions

1. Why do you see different stars during the different times of the year?

2. Which group of stars is always present in the night sky of the Northern Hemisphere?

3. What is the name of the North Star?

4. What is special about the star named Sirius?

5. What is a black hole?

6. What is a supernova?

7. Describe the three star categories.

8. What is a galaxy?

9. In which galaxy is the earth?

10. What is the shape of our galaxy?

11. What is a constellation?

12. How are constellations used today?

13. What is the difference between astronomy and astrology?

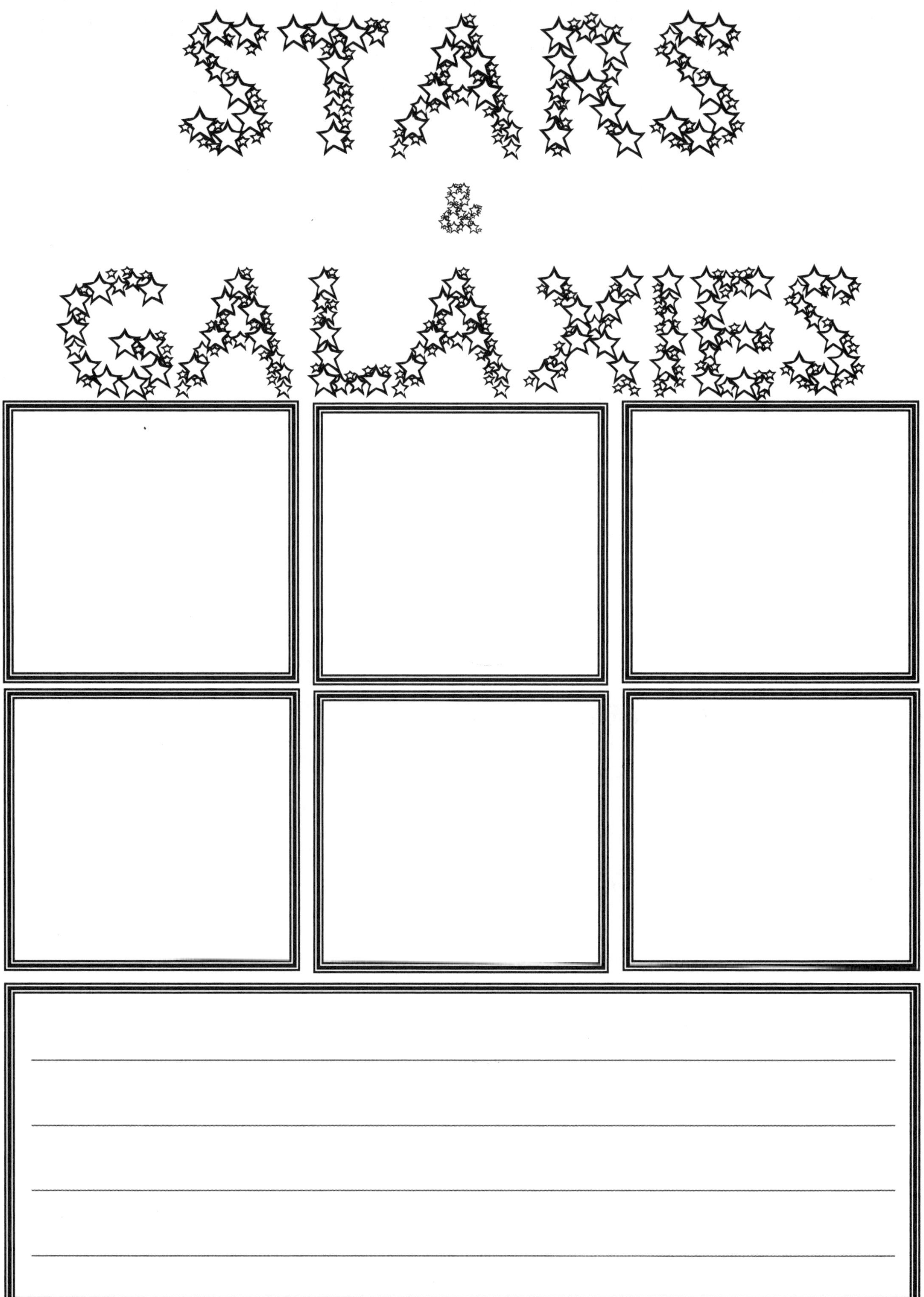
STARS
&
GALAXIES

The heavens are telling of the glory of God; and their expanse is declaring the work of His hands. Day to day pours forth speech, and night to night reveals knowledge.

Psalm 19:1-2

The heavens are telling of the glory of God; and their expanse is declaring the work of His hands. Day to day pours forth speech, and night to night reveals knowledge.

Psalm 19:1-2

Vocabulary Crossword

Lesson 13

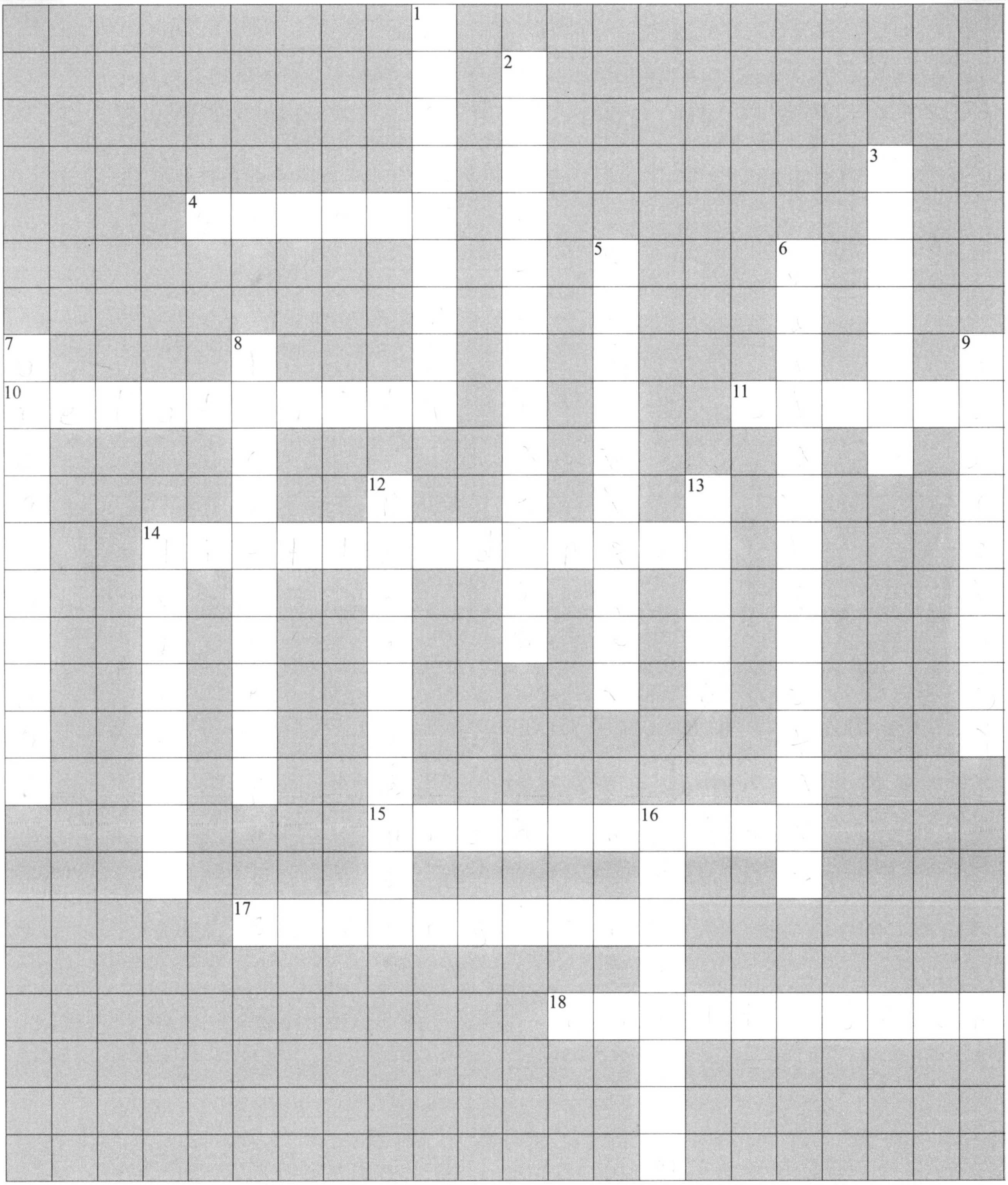

1
2
3
4
5
6
7
8
9
10
11
12
13
14
15
16
17
18

Vocabulary Crossword

Lesson 13

SIRIUS	LATITUDE	URSA MAJOR
GALAXY	BIG DIPPER	ASTERISM
BETELGEUSE	CONSTELLATION	NORTH STAR
ORION	SUPERGIANT	VARIABLE STARS
LIGHT YEAR	ASTROLOGY	LITTLE DIPPER
URSA MINOR	RELATIVITY	MILKY WAY
		POLARIS

Across

4. Billions of stars arranged together to form a single shape.
10. A type of science that tells us how certain parts of the universe can age at different rates.
11. The brightest star in the night's sky, found in the constellation Canis Major. (It's also called the Dog Star.)
14. A small asterism that looks like a small ladle or spoon with a handle. This asterism is in the constellation Ursa Minor. The star Polaris is also in this asterism **(put a space between the two words)**.
15. The Big Dipper is located in this constellation. Its name means "big bear" **(put a space between the two words)**.
17. What we call a star that is very large and bright, such as the star named Betelgeuse.
18. Another name for Polaris, visible in the Northern Hemisphere, around which all the other stars appear to rotate **(put a space between the two words)**.

Down

1. The galaxy in which our solar system is located **(put a space between the two words)**.
2. A group of stars that form a distinct pattern and is given a name. Each of these star patterns is used for navigation and to help scientists locate heavenly bodies and other things in the sky.
3. The name of the North Star, used for navigation throughout most of history because it does not move in the night's sky. It is found in the constellation Ursa Minor, and in the asterism The Little Dipper.
5. A large asterism that looks like a ladle or spoon with a long handle. This asterism is made up of the seven brightest stars inside the constellation Ursa Major **(put a space between the two words)**.
6. Stars that do not burn with a consistent brightness or energy **(put a space between the two words)**.
7. A small constellation containing the star Polaris. The name means "little bear." The Little Dipper is located in this constellation **(put a space between the two words)**.
8. The distance that light travels in one solar year **(put a space between the two words)**.
9. A false religion in which people put their faith in the stars, believing that star patterns can tell them the future and other things about life.
12. A bright supergiant star, located in the constellation of Orion. This star, though it is not the brightest in the night's sky, is larger than our entire solar system.
13. The constellation called "the Hunter," representing a man holding a shield.
14. An imaginary line that represents the distance, north or south, one is from the equator.
16. A set of stars that form a shape that is easy to recognize, but is not formally a constellation.

What I did:

What I learned:

STARS AND
GALAXIES

TAKE IT FURTHER

LESSON 13

Ancient Eye Test

The middle star in the Big Dipper's handle is a star called Mizar. There is a star lined up with Mizar named Alcor. They appear so close together that, to some, they can look like one star. In ancient days, these stars were sometimes used as an eye test. If you could see two separate stars, your eyesight was good; if not, you had poor eyesight.

On a clear night, go outside and look at the middle star in the handle of the Big Dipper. Is it one star, or can you see two? Look through some binoculars to get your answer.

Create a Constellation Myth

All of the constellations come with stories. The Ancient Greeks had stories for the constellations, as did the Ancient Indians, Native Americans and Chinese. Often these stories were quite similar to one another, and the constellations represented the same object or person, even though they don't look like the person or object they supposedly represent. These stories surrounded ancient mythical beings, people, animals and situations. For example, the story of Ursa Major and Ursa Minor revolves around the mythical heroes Jupiter and his wife, who turn a woman and her son into bears. If you feel up to it, research some of the constellation stories before doing this activity.

Choose a group of stars in the sky to create your own constellation. You can give it a name and make up a story that tells why the constellation is there in the sky and what it is doing.

Make a Star Wheel

A star wheel, or planisphere, is a device that helps you locate the stars in the sky during the different seasons. On the Internet, there are many sites that have printable star wheels you can make. Do a search for: "Make a Star Wheel" and you should find several to print and put together.

Books to Help with Finding Constellations

The Stars: A New Way to See Them by H.A. Rey

Find the Constellations by H.A. Rey

Fascinating Facts about Space Travel

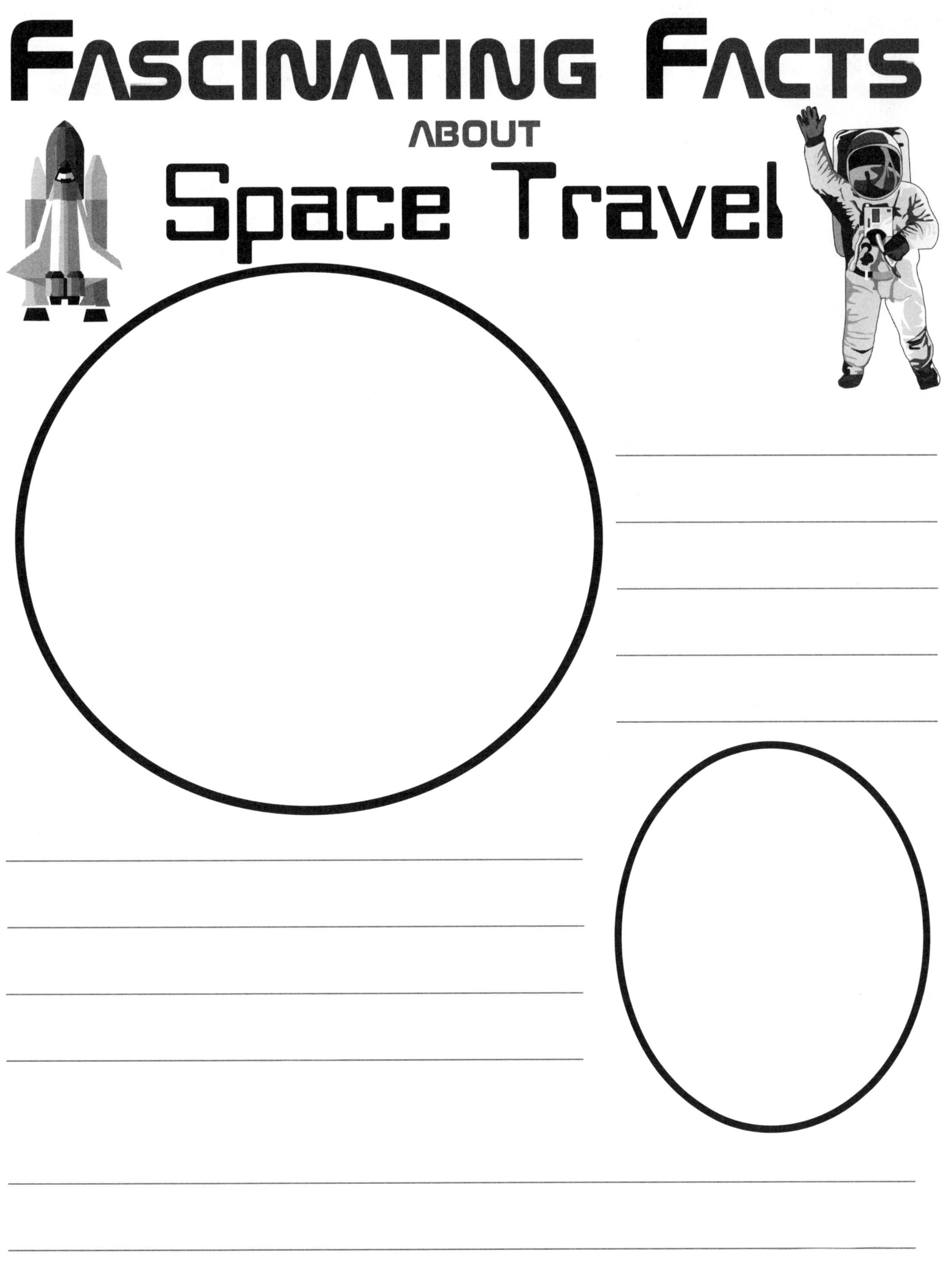

FASCINATING FACTS ABOUT Space Travel

Name ______________________________ Date ______________

What Do You Remember?
Lesson 14 Review Questions

1. What was the name of the first artificial satellite?

2. What was the race called between Russia and the United States?

3. Why was the United States worried about Russia's space program?

4. What did the United States do first?

5. What did Neil Armstrong say when he stepped on the moon?

6. What is the Space Station?

7. What is the name of the best space station?

8. What is the job of people who live on this space station?

9. What is life like on a space station?

10. How do you become an astronaut?

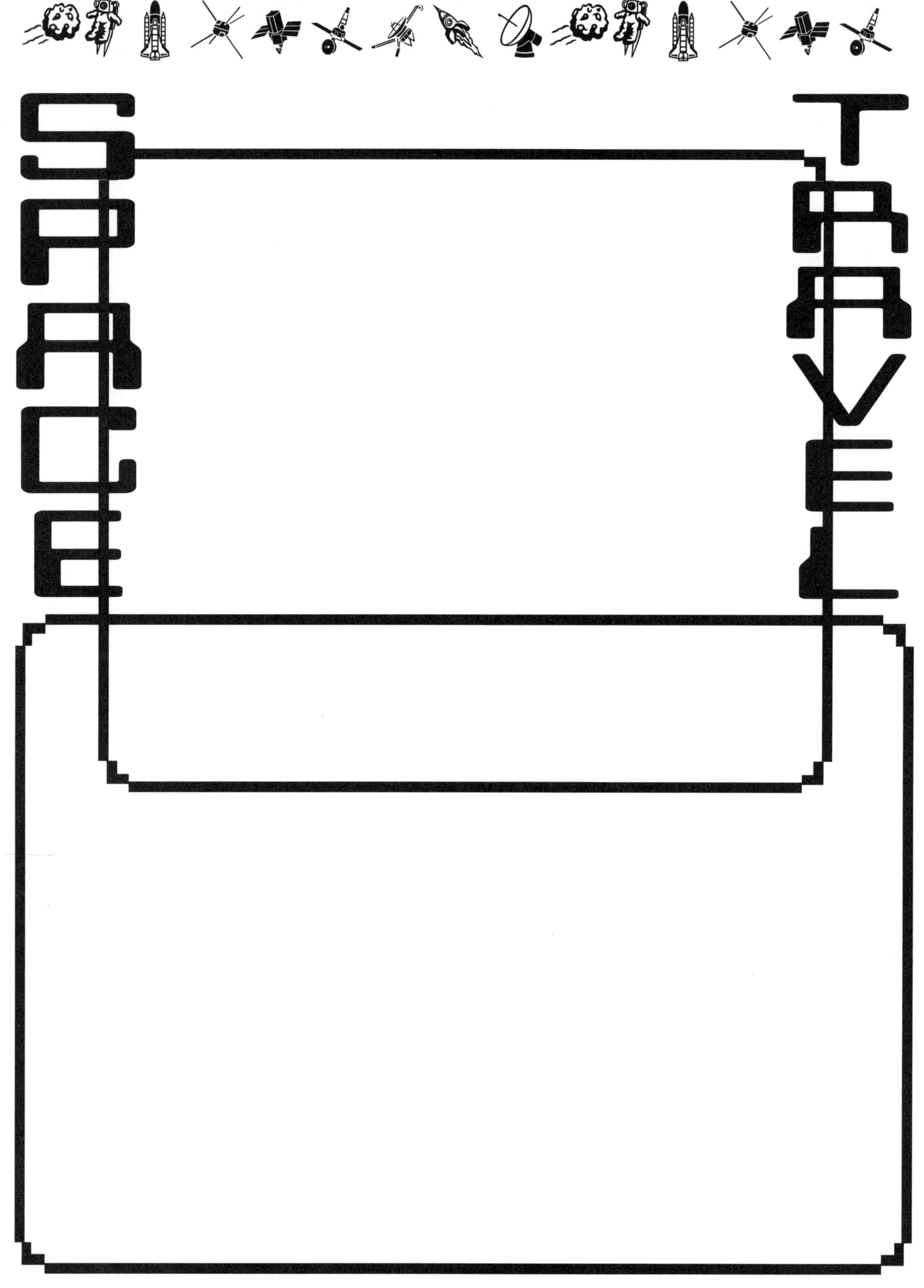
SPACE
TRAVEL

Let's Visit the Planets!

The day you leave the earth is your next birthday.	How old are you the day you leave?
You arrive on Mercury in 8 months.	How old are you when you get to Mercury? (your age + 8 months)
You arrive on Venus 4 months later.	How old are you when you reach Venus? (your last age + 4 months)
You arrive back on earth 4 months later and say hello to your family before you immediately set off for Mars.	How old are you when you reach earth? (your age + 4 months.)
You arrive on Mars in 7 months.	How old are you when you reach Mars?
You arrive on Jupiter in 3 years and 11 months.	How old are you when you reach Jupiter?
You arrive on Saturn 4 years and 7 months later.	How old are you when you reach Saturn?
You arrive on Uranus 10 years and 2 months later.	How old are you when you reach Uranus?
You arrive on Neptune 11 years and 7 months later.	How old are you when you reach Neptune?
You arrive on Pluto 10 years later.	How old are you when you reach Pluto?
It will take 40 years and 10 months to make it back home.	How old will you be when you get back?

When I consider Your heavens, the work of Your fingers, the moon and the stars, which You have ordained; what is man that You take thought of him, and the son of man that You care for him?

Psalm 8:3-4

When I consider Your heavens, the work of Your fingers, the moon and the stars, which You have ordained; what is man that You take thought of him, and the son of man that You care for him?

Psalm 8:3-4

Vocabulary Crossword

Lesson 14

ARMSTRONG
GODDARD
SPACE RACE
ASTRONAUTICS
COSMONAUT
SALYUT
SPUTNIK
EVA

Across

2. The name of the competition between the United States and Russia to advance their space technology **(put a space between the two words)**.
5. The man who, in 1919, studied how a person might get to the moon. He worked with rockets. He was called "Moon Man" by those who made fun of him.
6. The word Russians use to refer to human scientists that travel to space.
8. The first rocket that was launched into space. It was built by the Russians and began the space competition between the United States and Russia.

Down

1. Neil _____________________ was the first man to step on the moon.
3. The science of space flight.
4. Extravehicular activity, or a space walk.
7. The name of the first space station ever sent into space. This was a Russian space station.

My Space Travel Project

What I did:

What I learned:

Space Travel

Planets Review

TAKE IT FURTHER

LESSON 14

Visit a Planetarium

This might be a nice time to schedule a trip to a planetarium. A planetarium is a large, usually dome-shaped theater built to educate the public on the night's sky and astronomy. These are exciting and interesting theaters and you will enjoy the show; however, be forewarned that evolutionary content may be presented.

Many universities have a planetarium, as do most large cities. Look up the word "planetarium" on the Internet and find one that is near to where you live. You may want to call to schedule your visit.

Enter a Science Fair

If you have never participated in a science fair, this is a worthwhile activity. There are numerous resources to help you choose a science fair project. If you wish to do one based on astronomy, you can use one of the following books:

Janice Van Cleave's A+ Projects in Astronomy by Janice Van Cleave
Science Fair Projects: Flight, Space & Astronomy by Robert L. Bonnet
Astronomy and Space by Kelly Milner Halls

Name ______________________________ Date ______________

Exploring Creation with Astronomy Final Review

1. Which early astronomer discovered the moons of Jupiter through telescopes that he built himself?

2. Which early astronomer first believed that the earth revolved around the sun?

3. Name the order of the planets.

4. What is the four letter acronym that stands for the United States' space program?

5. What is the name of the dark spots that appear on the sun, which are cooler than the rest of the sun?

6. What are the names of the large bursts of fire that dart out from the sun?

7. How does the sun get its energy?

8. How does this process show us that life on earth could not have been present billions of years ago?

9. What is a solar eclipse?

10. What does the surface of Mercury look like?

11. When does it get cold on Mercury and why?

12. What is an unmanned spacecraft?

13. What is the atmosphere like on Venus?

14. When can we see Venus and Mercury in the sky?

15. What would happen if the earth were closer to the sun?

16. What would happen if the earth rotated more quickly?

17. What are the different phases of the moon?

18. Why do we have ocean tides?

19. What is a lunar eclipse?

20. Where is the largest volcano in our solar system?

21. Why is Mars called the Red Planet?

22. What is a comet?

23. What is an asteroid?

24. What is a meteoroid?

25. What is a meteor?

26. What is a meteorite?

27. Where is the asteroid belt?

28. Which planet protects the earth by pulling large comets into itself, thus keeping them from hitting the earth?

29. What is the Great Red Spot on Jupiter?

30. What are shepherd moons?

31. What are Saturn's rings made of?

32. Who discovered Uranus?

33. What type of gemstone is formed in the storms on Neptune?

34. What is the Kuiper belt?

35. Where is the Kuiper belt located?

36. What is unusual about Pluto's moon?

37. Why is Pluto's orbit more like a comet than a planet?

38. What is a constellation?

39. How are constellations used today?

40. What is Polaris?

41. What are supernovas?

42. Name the four kinds of galaxies.

43. What is our galaxy called?

44. What kind of galaxy is it?

45. What are Ursa Major and Ursa Minor? Where are they located in the night's sky?

46. What is the name of the first rocket, built by the Russians, that was sent into space?

47. What was the competition called between the Russians and Americans to create space technology?

48. What is the name of the space station that orbits the earth and is shared by many countries?

49. Name at least one moon, besides the earth's moon, in our solar system.

50. What did Neil Armstrong say when he stepped on the moon?

Vocabulary Solutions

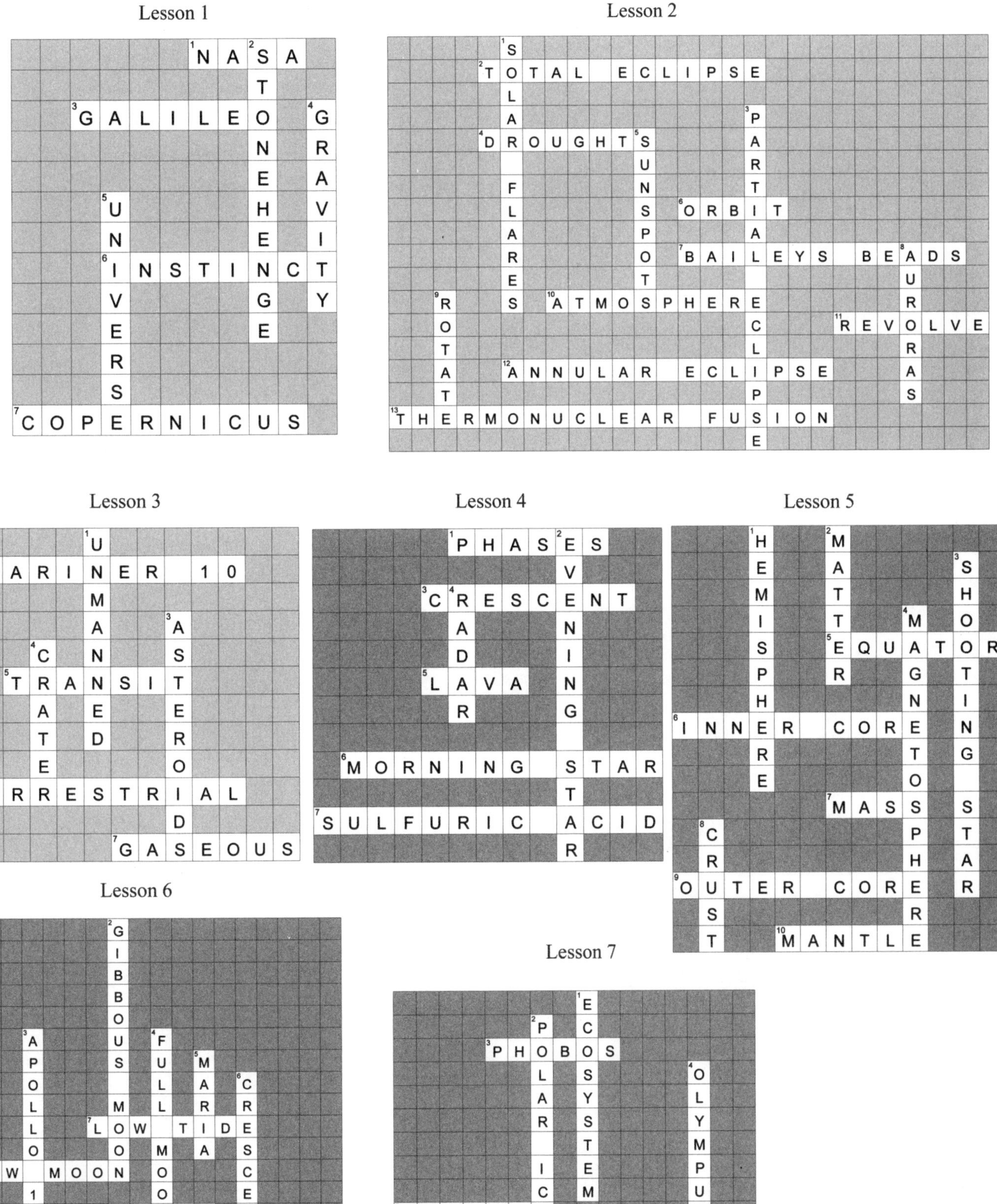

Lesson 8

Lesson 9

Lesson 10

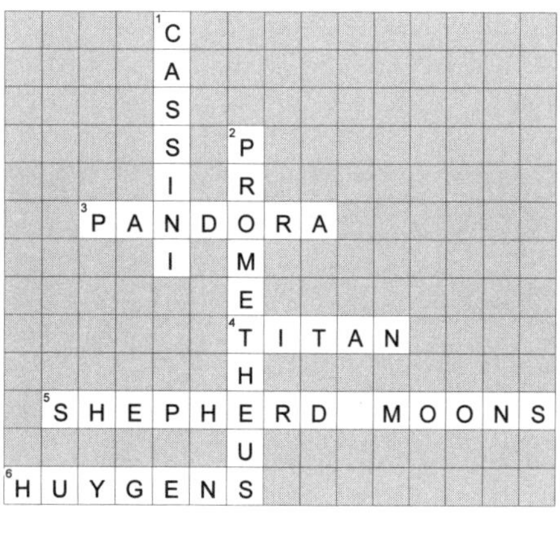

Lesson 11

Lesson 12

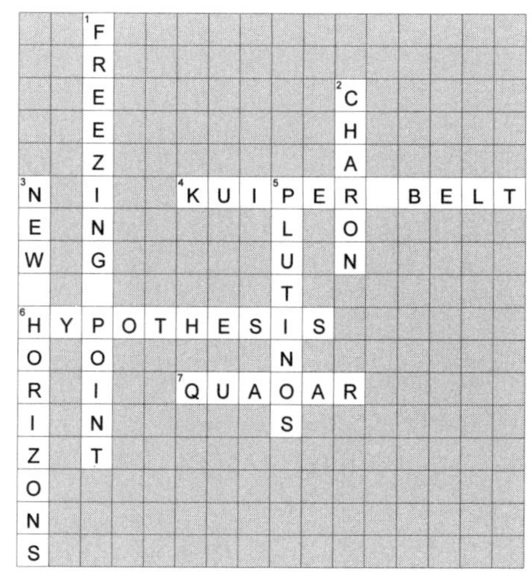

Lesson 13

1 MILKY WAY
2 CONSTELLATION
3 POLARIS
4 GALAXY
5 BIG DIPPER
6 VARIABLE STARS
7 URSA MINOR
8 LIGHT YEAR
9 ASTROLOGY
10 RELATIVITY
11 SIRIUS
12 BETELGEUSE
13 ORION
14 LITTLE DIPPER
LATITUDE
15 URSA MAJOR
16 ASTERISM
17 SUPERGIANT
18 NORTH STAR

Lesson 14

1 ARMSTRONG
2 SPACE RACE
3 ASTRONAUTICS
4 EVA
5 GODDARD
6 COSMONAUT
7 SALYUT
8 SPUTNIK

Final Review Solutions

1. Galileo
2. Copernicus
3. Mercury, Venus, Earth, Mars, Jupiter, Saturn, Uranus, Neptune
4. NASA
5. Sunspots
6. Solar flares
7. Thermonuclear fusion
8. Over time, thermonuclear fusion would cause the sun to burn brighter. This tells us that billions of years ago, the sun would have been much dimmer-too dim to support life.
9. When the moon passes between the earth and the sun
10. It has many impact craters.
11. It gets cold at night. It does this because Mercury does not have an atmosphere to retain heat, and it is also night for many days.
12. A spacecraft that does not have a man on it
13. Venus has thick acidic clouds that retain heat on the planet.
14. Shortly after sunset or shortly before sunrise
15. The earth would be too hot to support life.
16. The earth would have many more hurricanes and strong winds.
17. New, Gibbous, Crescent, Half, Full
18. Because the moon's gravity pulls on the ocean, causing it to bulge
19. When the earth is between the moon and the sun
20. Mars
21. Because it has red dirt (made of rusted iron)
22. A large ball of ice, dirt and rock that orbits the sun
23. A very large space rock
24. A space rock that is smaller than an asteroid
25. A space rock that has entered the earth's atmosphere
26. A space rock that has hit the earth
27. Between Mars and Jupiter
28. Jupiter
29. An enormous storm that has been raging for hundreds of years
30. Moons that keep Saturn's rings together
31. Rocks, boulders and moons
32. A brother and sister, William and Caroline Herschel
33. Diamond
34. A large belt of asteroids and comets
35. Outside of our solar system, beyond Pluto
36. Compared to the size of the planet it orbits, it is very large.
37. Because it is elliptical and inclined
38. A group of stars that seem to form the shape of a person or object
39. Constellations are used in astronomy to locate objects in the sky.
40. The North Star or the star around which all the others appear to orbit
41. Exploding stars
42. Spiral, lenticular, elliptical, and irregular
43. The Milky Way
44. Spiral
45. They are constellations that are shaped like a big bear and a little bear. The Little Dipper is a part of Ursa Minor and the Big Dipper is part of Ursa Major. The North Star is at the end of the Little Dipper's "handle," and the two stars at the end of the Big Dipper's "bowl" point to the North Star.
46. Sputnik
47. Space Race
48. International Space Station
49. Answers will vary
50. "That's one small step for man, one giant leap for mankind."

My Astronomy Field Trip

Place: **Date:**

The purpose of this field trip:

What I saw/ did on this trip:

What I learned:

My favorite part:

My Astronomy Field Trip

Place: **Date:**

The purpose of this field trip:

What I saw/ did on this trip:

What I learned:

My favorite part:

CREATION CONFIRMATION MINI BOOK

(Instructions on back)

Creation Confirmation

It's important to remember all you've learned about God and Creation in this course. This Creation Confirmation Book will enable you to record and recall your learning.

Instructions:

1. Cut out the Creation Confirmation Book rectangles on pages 1 and 3 along the dotted lines. **Do not cut the gold fold lines!**
2. Fold the pages along the gold lines.
3. Place the pages inside the purple cover of the book.
4. Open the book to the middle and staple it along the center.
5. As you work through each lesson of the astronomy course, write down what you learn about God, the Bible and Creation.
6. Keep your Creation Confirmation Book inside your astronomy book as a book mark and a reminder to write down the things you learn about God.

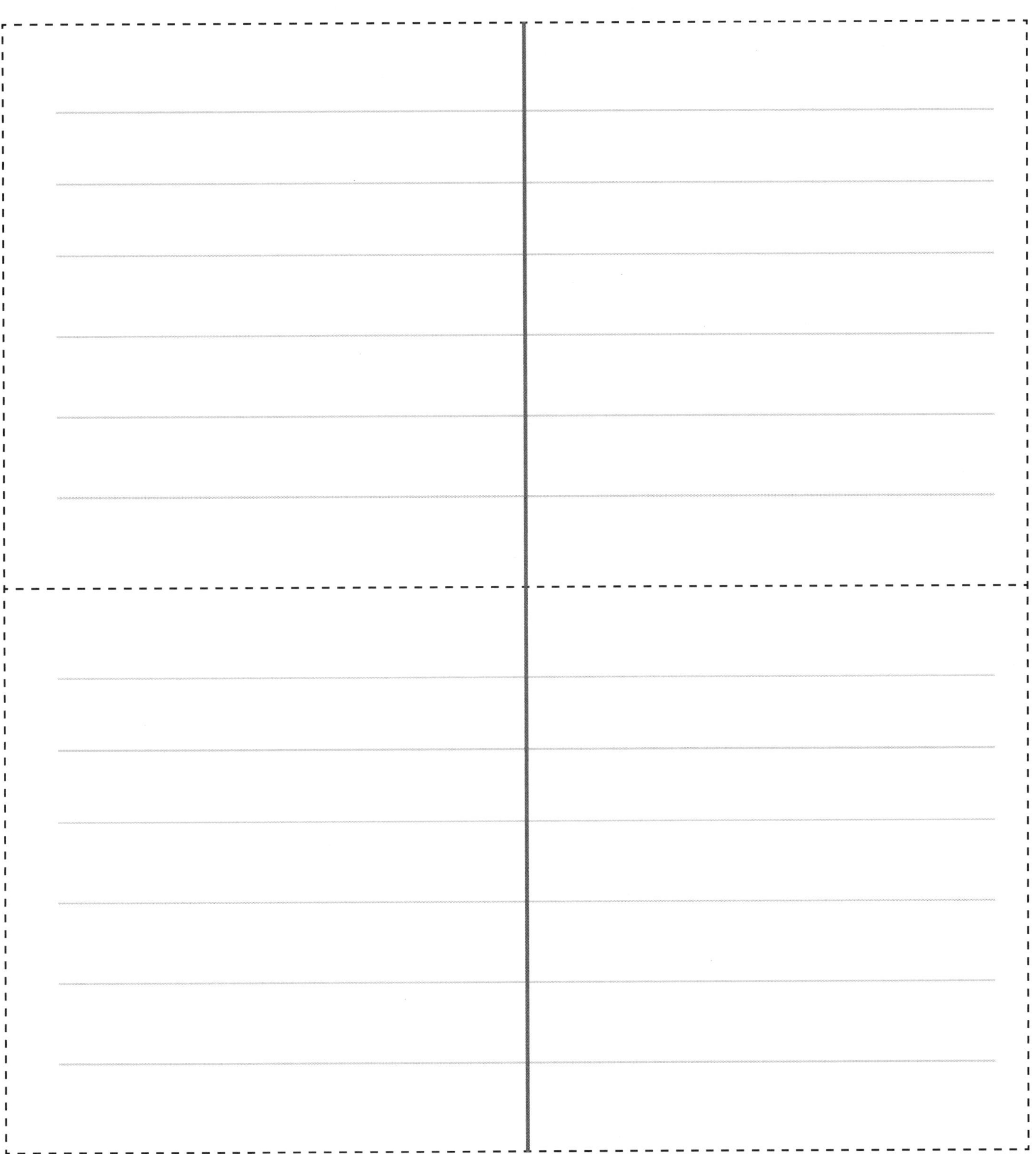

EXTRA MINI BOOKS

Glue this side to your paste page.

If you would like to record any additional information not included in the other miniature books, here are a few extra miniature books for you to use.

Instructions:

1. Cut out the three mini book covers along the dotted lines. **Do not cut the gold fold lines!**
2. Fold the covers in half along the gold fold lines.
3. Have fun recording all the interesting facts you learn about astronomy!

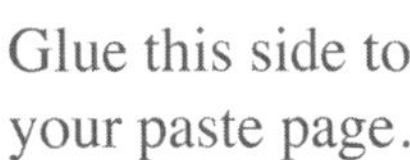

Glue this side to your paste page.

Glue this side to your paste page.

WHAT IS ASTRONOMY? MATCHBOOK

This is the matchbook cover that will hold all your square pages.

Instructions:

1. Cut out the matchbook cover along the dotted lines. **Do not cut the blue fold lines!**
2. Fold along the blue lines so that the large Solar System flap and the small flap face outward in the same direction.
3. Cut out all eight squares on this page and the next and fill in the information you learned about astronomy.
4. Lift the large flap and place all the pages you created under the small flap.
5. With the large cover flap open and your eight pages under the small flap, staple your matchbook on the white line that crosses the center of the small flap. This will hold all your pages inside. **Do not staple the cover closed!**
6. Fold the large flap down and tuck it into the small flap, like a matchbook.
7. Glue this side (with these words) onto the "What is Astronomy?" paste page.

Galileo

NASA

Constellations

Nicolas Copernicus

Stonehenge

Natural Satellite

Yellow Circle

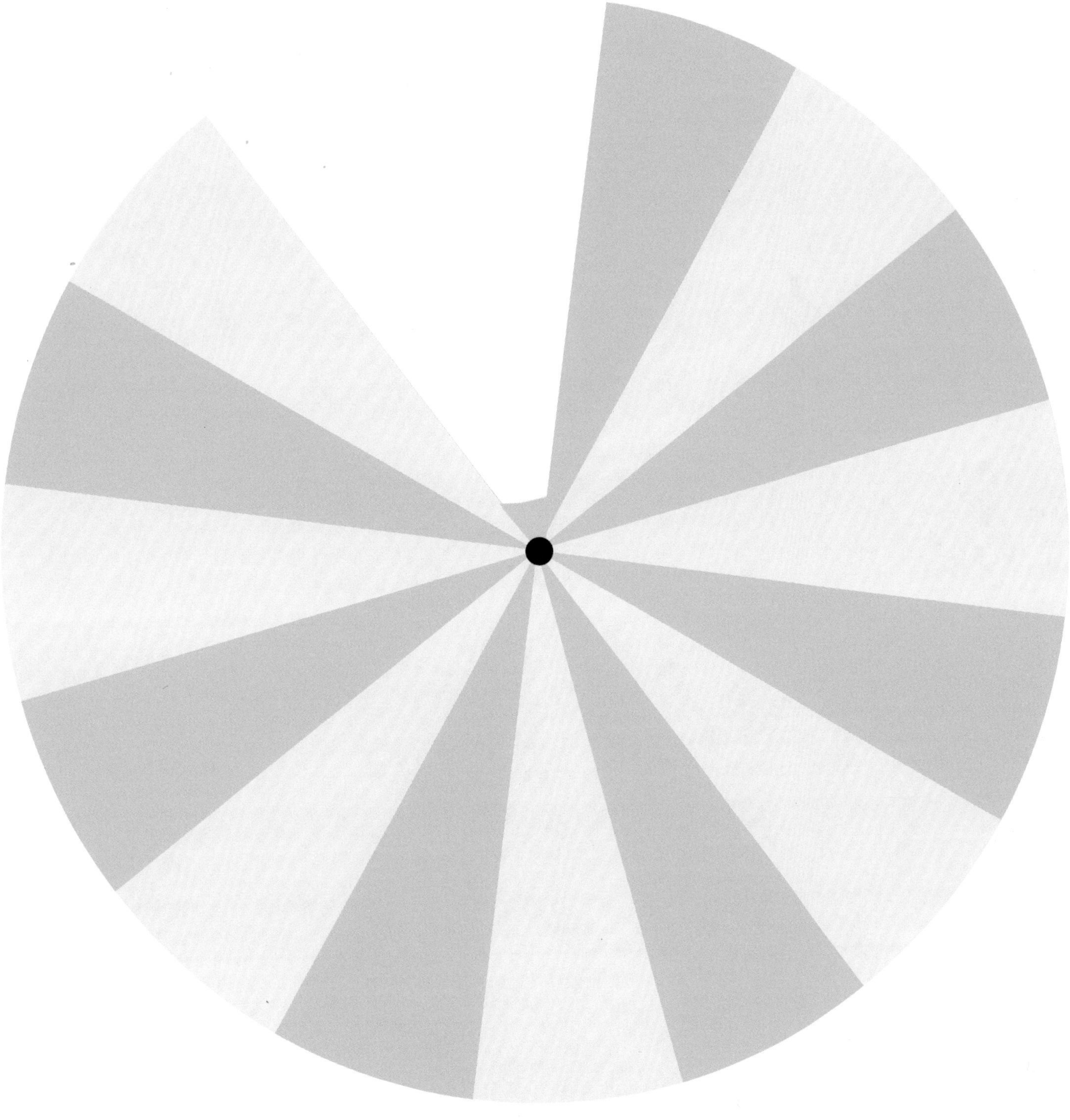

Instructions:

1. In the empty triangle below each topic, write a fact you learned about that topic listed in the Fact Circle.
2. Cut out the Fact Circle and the Yellow Circle. Be certain to cut out the white triangle in the Yellow Circle.
4. Place the Yellow Circle on top of the Fact Circle and insert a brass fastener in the center to secure the two circles.
5. Dab glue on the bottom of the Fact Circle and glue your Sun Wheel onto the "Sun" paste page.
6. Turn the Yellow Circle around to reveal the different facts about each topic.

Fact Circle

Rainbow Mini Book Instructions:

1. Cut out the rainbow along the outside dotted lines and fold it in half so that the words appear on the outside.
2. Cut out the small circle in the center while it is folded in half (you will cut a semicircle, which will reveal a full circle when the rainbow opens).
3. Open the rainbow book and write what you learned about color on the inside.
4. Affix your rainbow book onto your "Sun" paste page.

Eclipse Mini Book Instructions:

1. Cut out the Solar Eclipse book around the half-circles and along the dotted lines. **Do not cut the gold fold lines!**
2. Fold the orange and black semi-circles inward along the gold lines.
3. Open the flaps and draw an illustration of a solar eclipse with the earth, moon and sun on the inside.
4. Write down what you learned about total eclipse, annular eclipse and a partial eclipse on the lines.
5. Glue the bottom side of your Solar Eclipse book onto your "Sun" paste page.

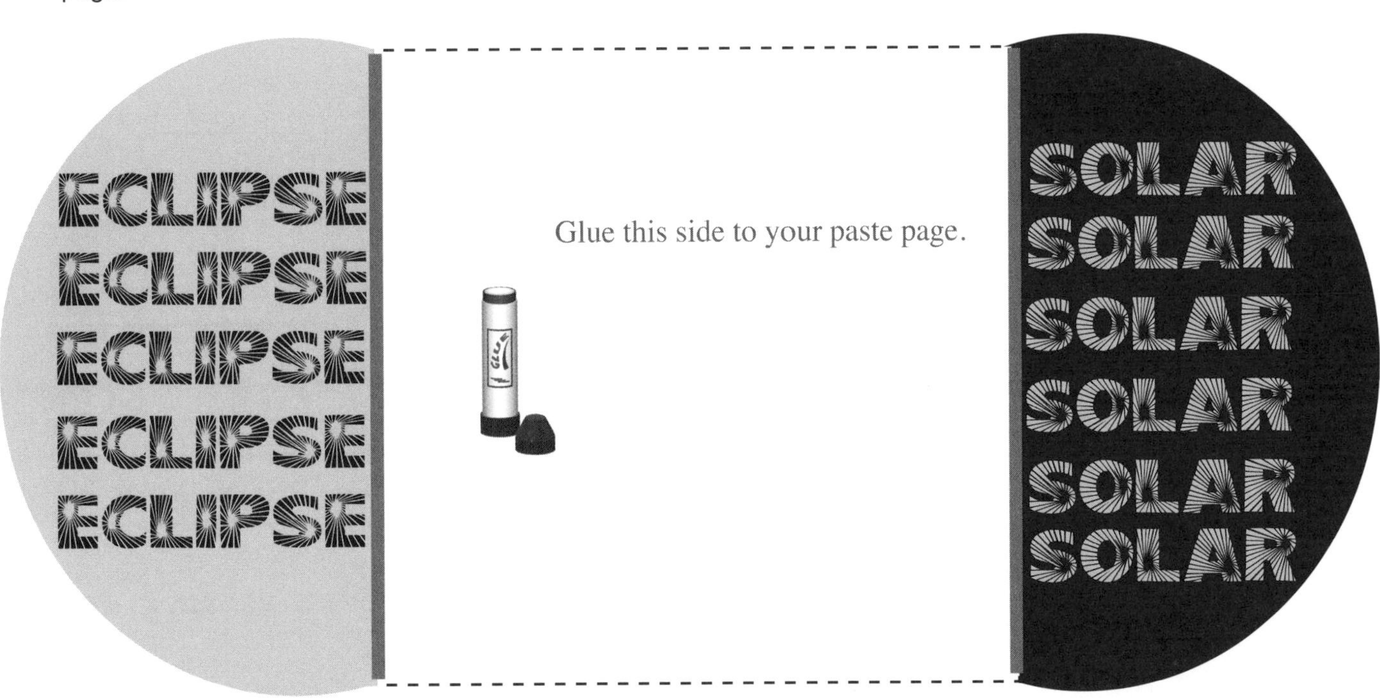

MERCURY MINI BOOKS

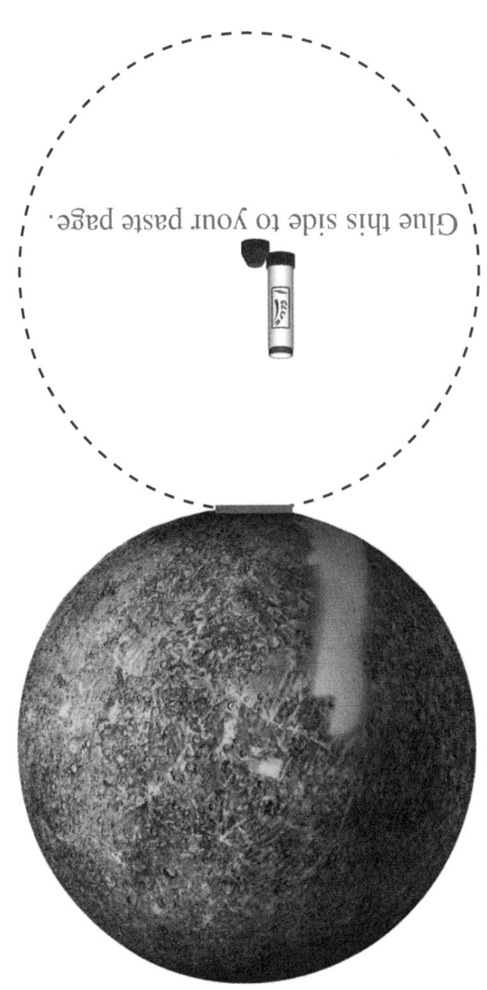

Instructions:

1. Cut out your Mercury mini books along the dotted lines. **Do not cut the gold fold lines!** Fold your books in half.
2. Write facts you learned about Mercury on the inside lines.
3. Glue your mini books to your "Mercury" paste page.

Glue this side to your paste page.

VENUS VOLCANO

Instructions:

1. Cut out the Venus volcano.
2. Cut an opening in the top of the volcano along the white dotted line. Be careful not to cut into the volcano. Make sure you cut the entire dotted line. You might use scissors to poke a hole in the white line and then cut the opening with the scissors inserted.
3. Turn the volcano over and dab glue around the outside edges only. **Do not rub glue all over the volcano. Be careful not to glue the opening at the top closed.**
4. Glue your volcano to the "Venus" paste page. Be careful not to glue the slit closed.
5. Follow the directions on the next two pages to make the clouds for your volcano.

Instructions:

1. Cut out the clouds (one on this page and four on the next). **Do not cut the gold fold lines!**
2. Fold each cloud along the solid gold line with the words facing outside.
3. Inside each cloud, write the information you've learned about the topic listed on the outside of the cloud.
4. Cut out the strips on this page along the dotted lines.
5. Dab glue on the glue squares (located on the back of each cloud) and affix the clouds to the strips. Let the glue dry.
6. Insert the strips (from smallest to largest) at an angle into the volcano's slit opening.
7. Pull up on each cloud and open to read what you've learned about Venus.

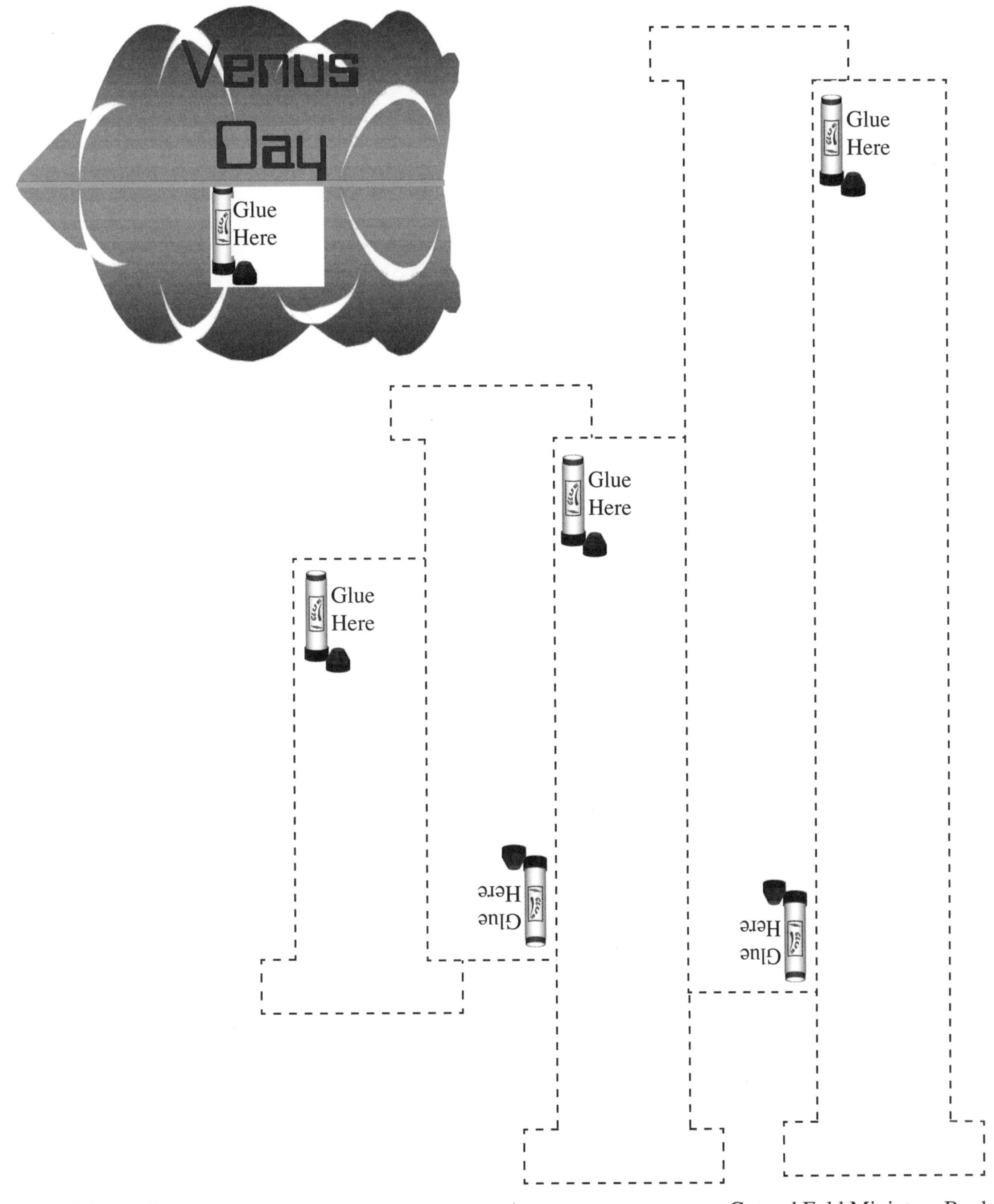

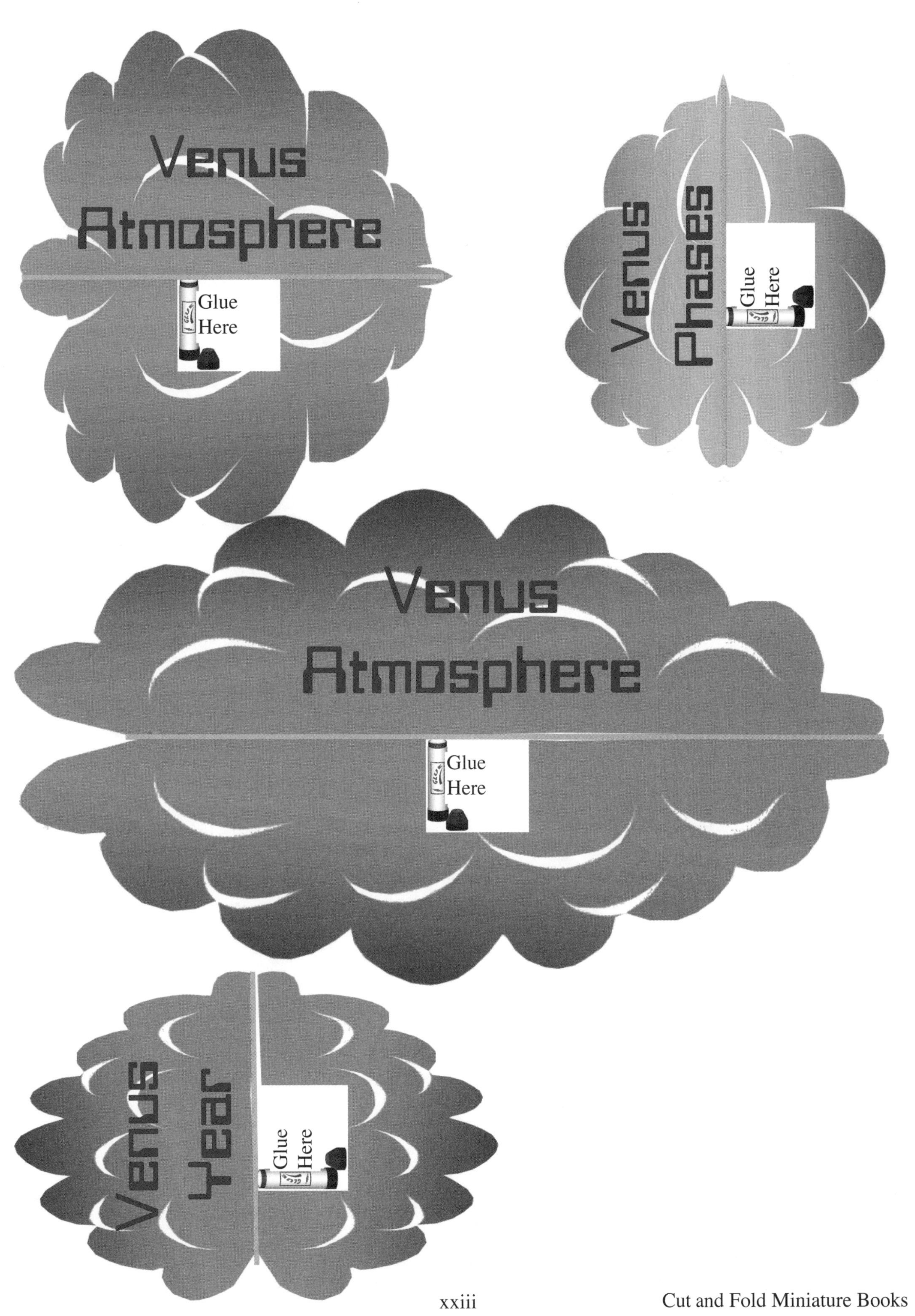
Venus
Atmosphere
Glue
Here
Venus
Phases
Glue
Here
Venus
Atmosphere
Glue
Here
Venus
Year
Glue
Here

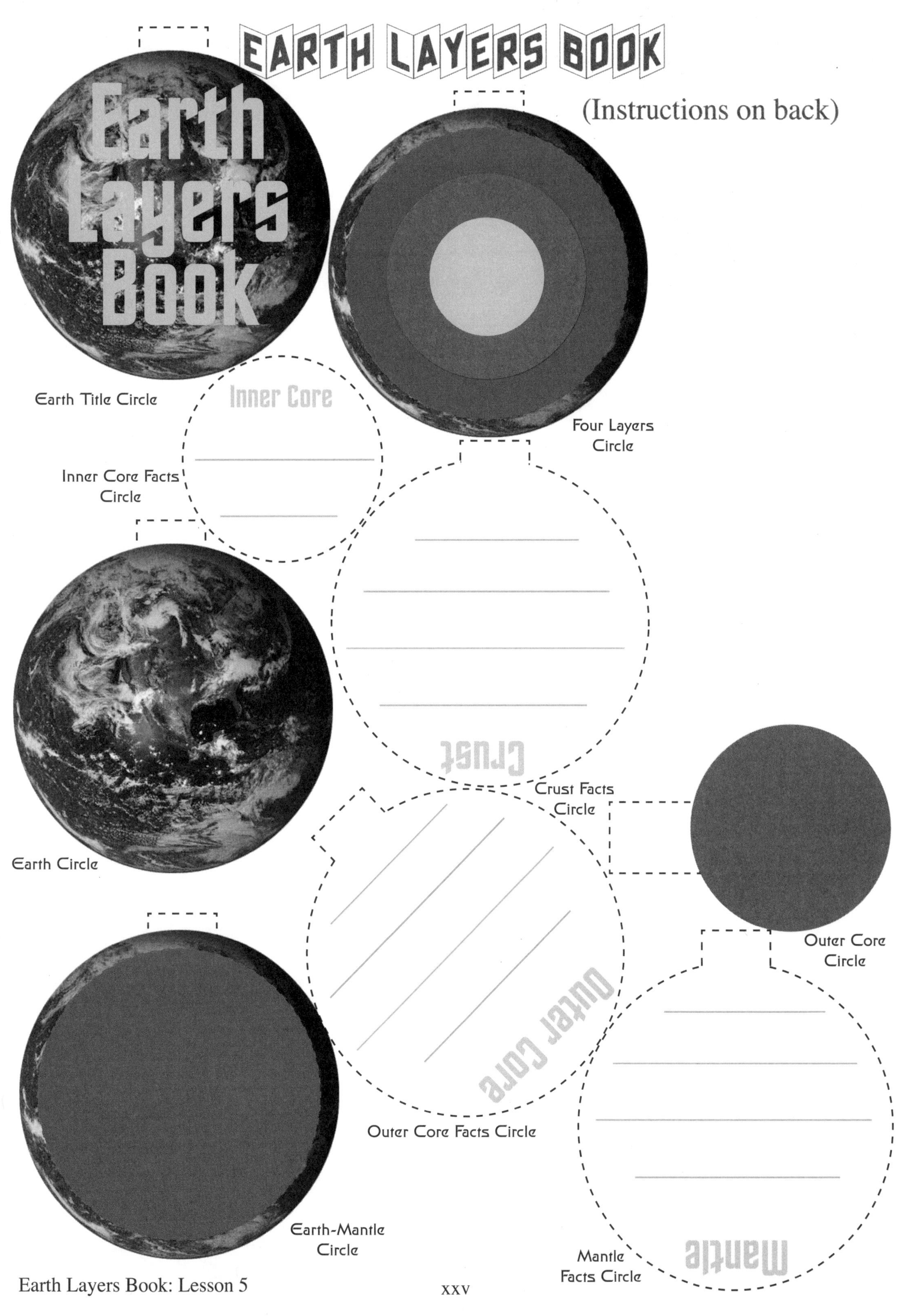
EARTH LAYERS BOOK
(Instructions on back)
Earth Layers Book
Earth Title Circle
Four Layers Circle
Inner Core
Inner Core Facts Circle
Crust
Crust Facts Circle
Earth Circle
Outer Core Circle
Outer Core
Outer Core Facts Circle
Earth-Mantle Circle
Mantle
Mantle Facts Circle

Instructions:

1. Cut out each circle with the tabs attached.
2. Write down the information you've learned on the lines under each topic, including: where the layer is located inside the earth (how far down) and of what materials it is made (Magma, Nickel).
3. Glue the Crust Facts Circle upside down to the Earth Title Circle.
4. Glue the Mantle Facts Circle upside down to the Earth Circle.
5. Glue the Outer Core Facts Circle upside down to the Earth-Mantle Circle.
6. Glue the Inner Core Facts Circle upside down to the bottom of the Outer Core Circle.
7. Glue the back of the Four Layers Circle onto the right hand side of your "Earth" paste page (leaving room for your Earth Lift Book).
8. Stack the circles on top of the Four Layers Circle in the correct order with the picture facing up and the facts facing down (Inner Core, Outer Core, Mantle, Crust); and glue them together on the rectangle tabs at the top.
9. Fold the tabs back as you lift each page of your Earth Layers Book. Each layer should display the definition and written information on the tab above the layer.

EARTH LIFT BOOK

Instructions:

1. Cut out the large rectangle along the outer dotted lines. **Do not cut the green fold line! Do not cut the divider lines at this time.**
2. Fold the rectangle along the solid green line so that the words face outward.
3. Cut along the divider dotted lines to create eight flaps. Under each flap, write how each feature listed makes the earth habitable. If you have room, also write what would happen if the earth did not have that perfect feature.
4. Lift the flaps to enjoy reading about the earth.
5. Glue this side of the book onto the "Earth" paste page.

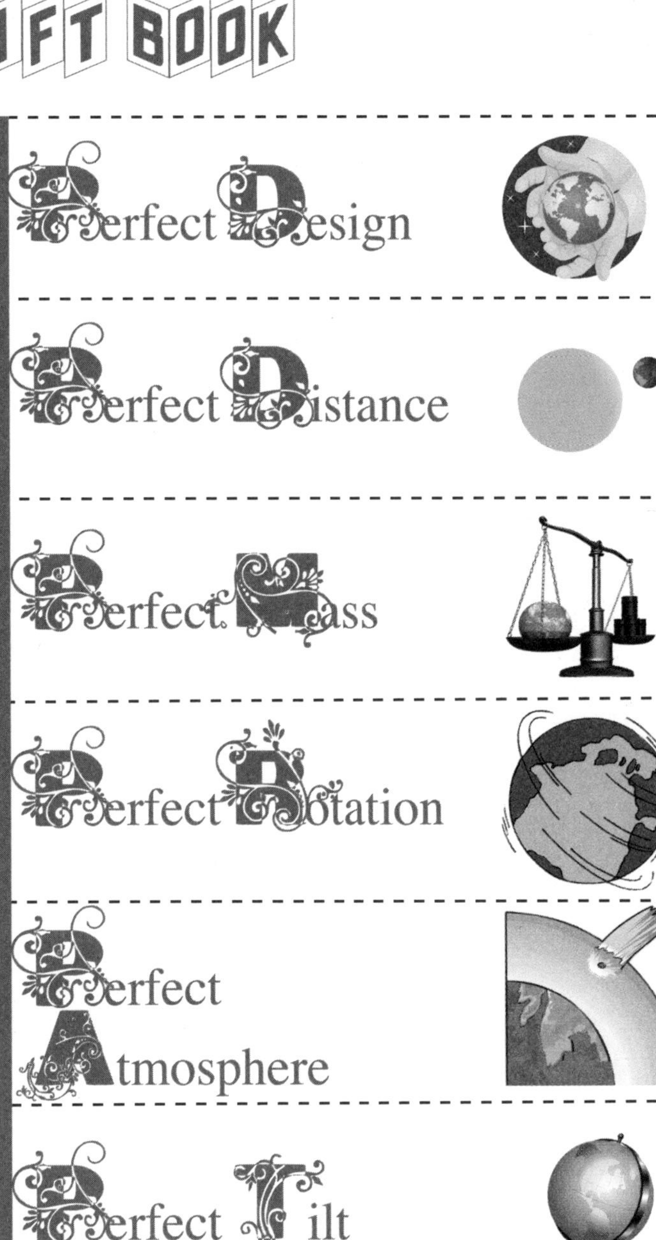

Perfect Design

Perfect Distance

Perfect Mass

Perfect Rotation

Perfect Atmosphere

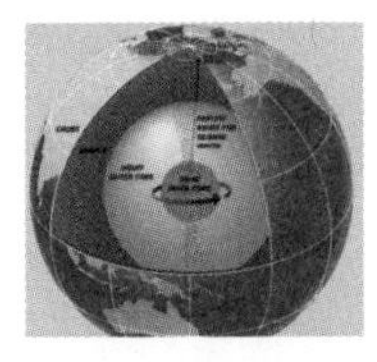

MOON LAYERED BOOK

(Instructions on next page)

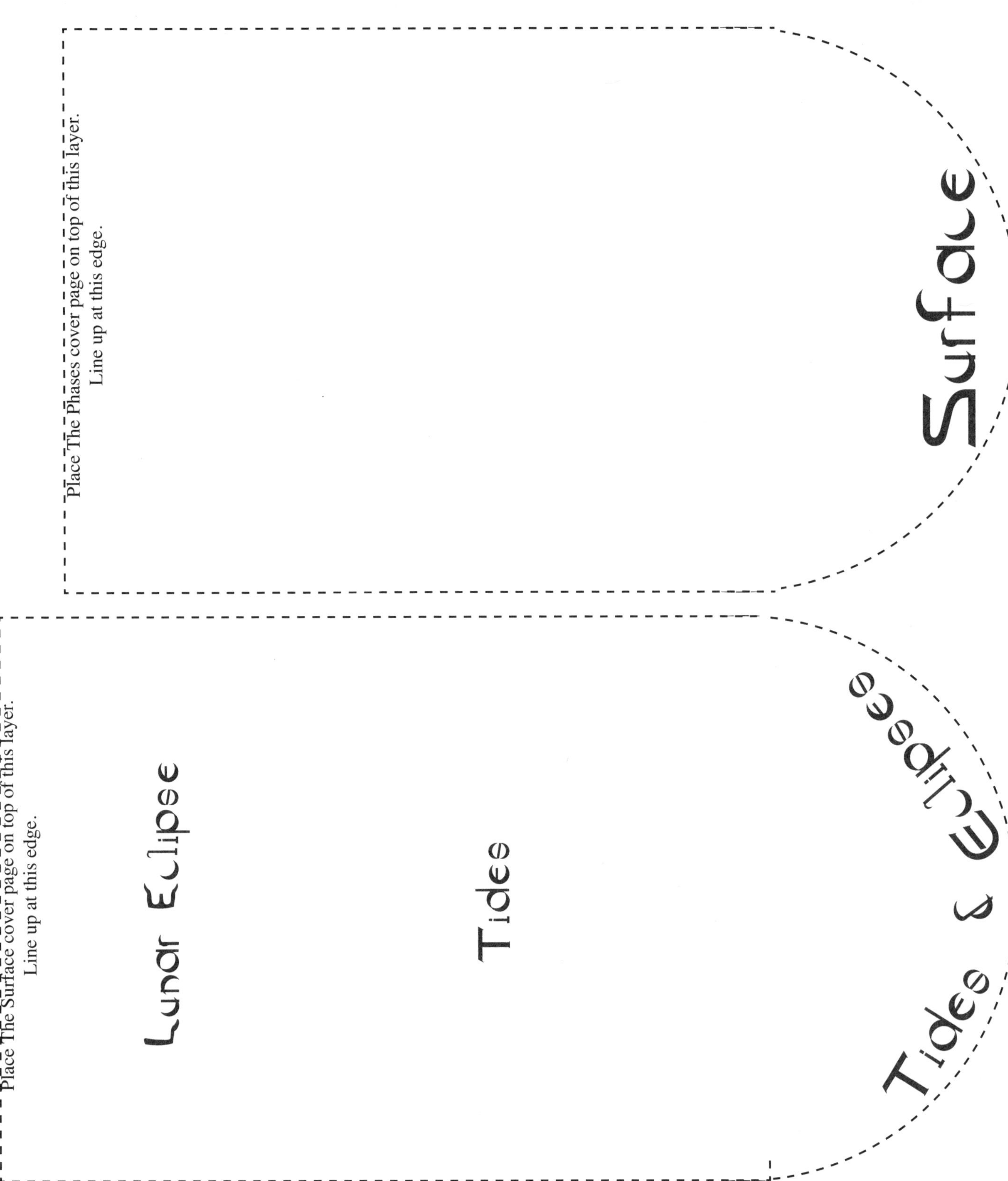

Instructions:

1. Cut out the four moon pages (two on this page and two on the next) along the dotted lines.
2. Write or draw the information requested on each page.
3. Stack the moon pages on top of one another beginning with the longest on the bottom and ending with the short "Moon" title page on top.
4. Staple your pages together along the top straight edge above the title "The Moon."
5. Glue your Moon Book onto your "Moon" paste page and lift the pages to enjoy reading what you learned about the moon.

MARS WHEELS

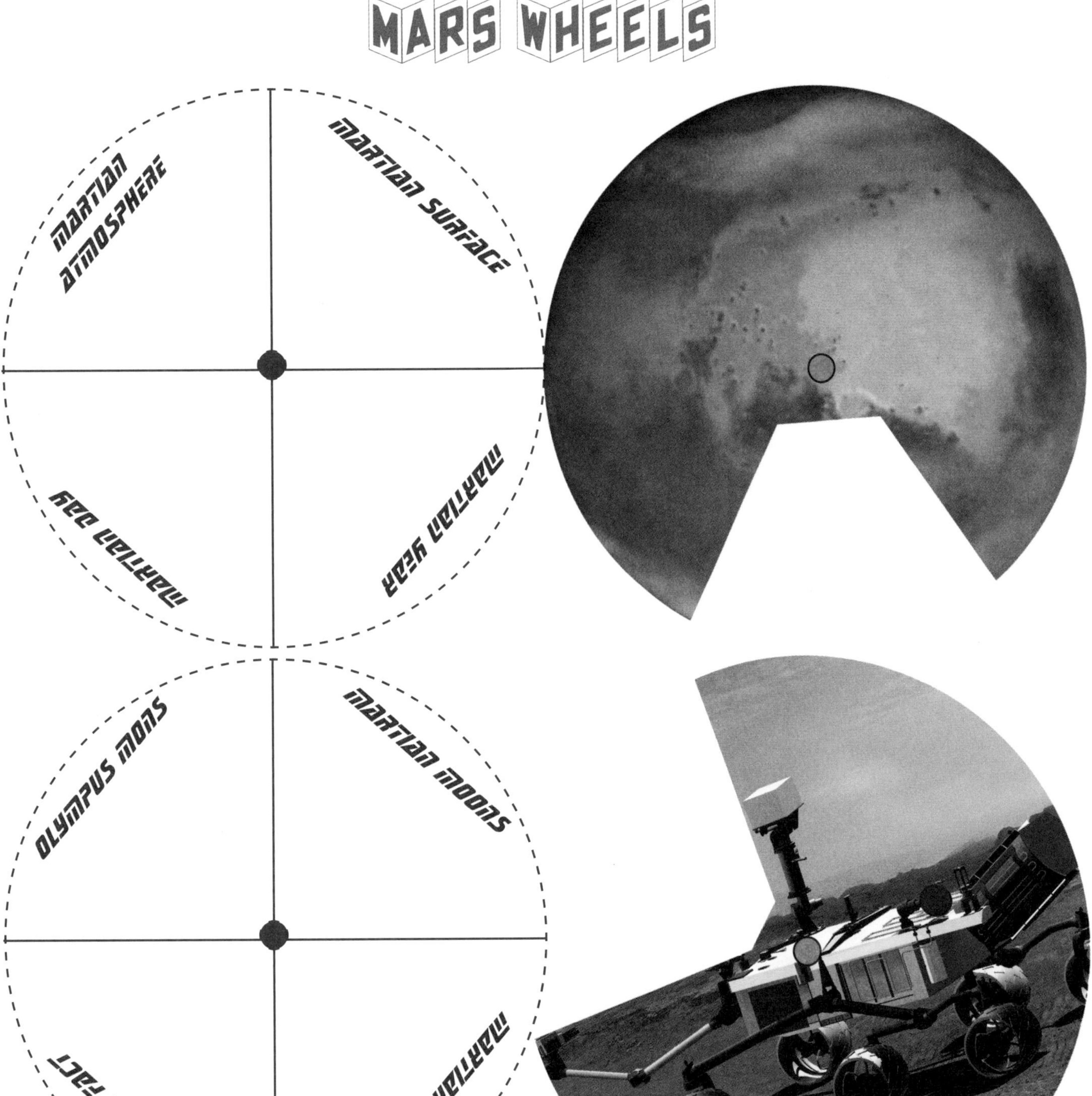

Instructions:

1. Write an interesting fact you learned under the title in each fact wheel.
2. Cut out all four circles, along with the cutout in the picture circles.
3. Place each picture circle on top of a fact wheel circle.
4. Secure the top circle to the bottom circle by placing a brass fastener in the center of each circle.
5. Turn the wheel to reveal the facts about Mars.
6. Glue the bottom of each fact wheel to your "Mars" paste page.

SPACE ROCKS LAYERED BOOK

Glue the Space Rocks Title Page Here

What are Asteroids?

What is the Asteroid Belt?

ASTEROIDS

Instructions:

1. Write down facts you learned under each title listed on the rectangle pages of your layered book.
2. Cut out all four rectangle pages (Space Rocks, Asteroids, Meteors, Comets).
3. Stack the pages on top of each other with the smallest page on top.
4. Line the pages up at the top with the title of each page showing at the bottom.
5. Staple the pages along the top to secure them together.
6. Glue your layered book onto the "Space Rocks" paste page.
7. Lift the layers to read about space rocks.

Glue the Asteroids Page Here

What are Meteoroids?

What are Meteors?

What are Meteorites?

What are Shooting Stars?

METEORS

Glue the Meteors Page Here

What are Comets?

Draw a Comet's Orbit

How are Comets Evidence for a Creation?

COMETS

JUPITER SHUTTER BOOK

Glue this side to your paste page.

Instructions:

1. Cut out the Jupiter Shutter Book rectangle. **Do not cut the gold fold lines!**
2. Fold the flaps of the shutter book inward so that the image meets, revealing the complete planet of Jupiter when the book is shut.
3. Fill in facts and information you learned about Jupiter on the lines inside the book.
4. Glue the back down onto your "Jupiter" paste page.

Galilean Moons

Europa

Io

Callisto

Ganymede

Jupiter Facts

Great Red Spot

Shoemaker-Levy

SATURN POCKET BOOK

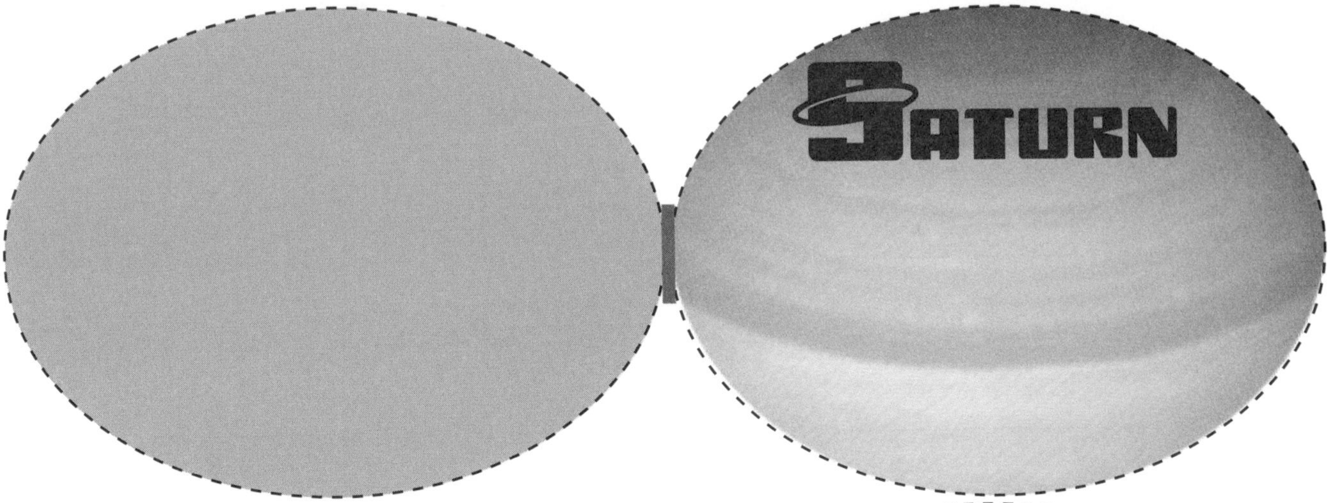

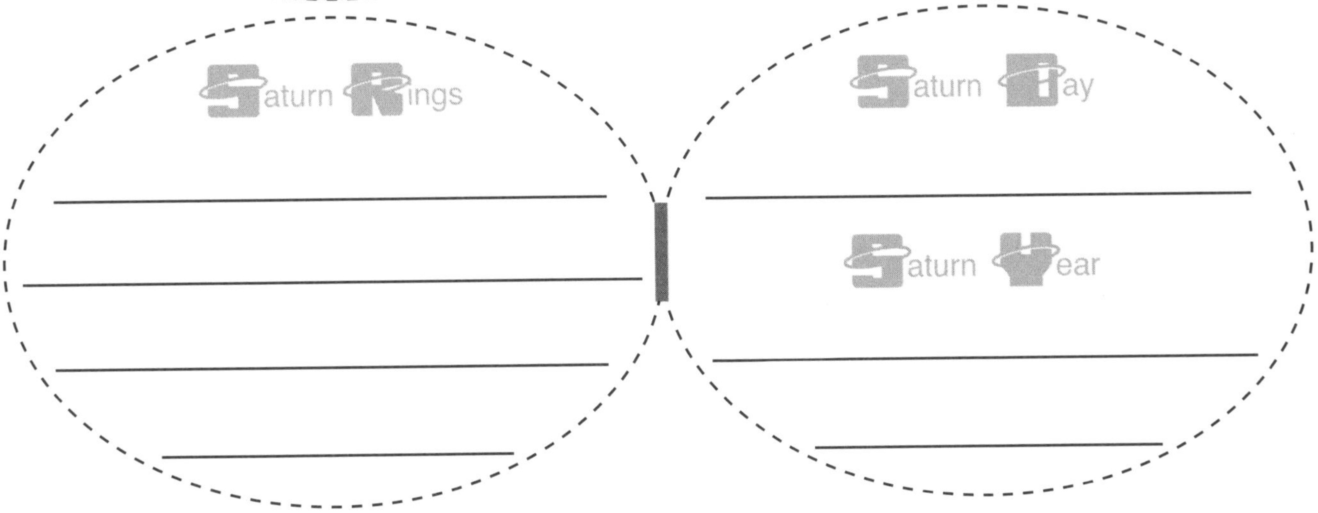

Saturn

Saturn Rings

Saturn Day

Saturn Year

Instructions:

1. Cut out the Saturn Pocket. Create an opening by cutting out the white oval inside Saturn's rings. This is the pocket where you will insert your Saturn Pocket Book.
2. Place glue **on the outside edges only** of your Saturn Pocket.
3. Glue the Saturn Pocket to your "Saturn" paste page being certain not to glue the center opening closed.
4. Cut out the two sets of attached ovals. **Be certain not to cut the gold fold lines!**
5. Fold the ovals at the gold fold lines and place the lined pages inside the cover pages to make a single book.
6. Staple your book on the center line.
7. Write all the facts you learned about Saturn on the lines inside your book.
8. Place your book inside the Saturn Pocket on your "Saturn" paste page.

Saturn Facts

Saturn Facts

Saturn Facts

Saturn Facts

URANUS AND NEPTUNE POP UP BOOKS

Neptune

Uranus

Instructions:

1. Cut out the two rectangles on this page. **Do not cut the grey fold lines!**
2. Write down what you learned about each planet on the lines provided. Fold the rectangles inward along the center grey fold line so that the titles are not visible.
3. Make four small cuts along the dashed lines in the center of each rectangle.
4. Open the paper up and gently pull each pop-up tab forward.
5. Crease the pop-up tabs with your fingers. Close the book to crease the pop-up tabs along the center line so that they are creased outward.
6. Cut out the two colored rectangle covers and the planets on page xlv, being careful with Uranus' rings.
7. Fold the covers inward so that the titles are on the outside. Glue them to the outside of your lined rectangles to form the book cover.
8. Glue your planets to the front of the pop-up tabs inside each book.
9. Glue your pop-up books to your "Uranus and Neptune" paste page.
10. Open your books to see your planets pop up, and enjoy reading all about Uranus and Neptune.

These are the covers for your pop-up books. Fold them inward along the center lines and glue them to the outside of your pop-up pages.

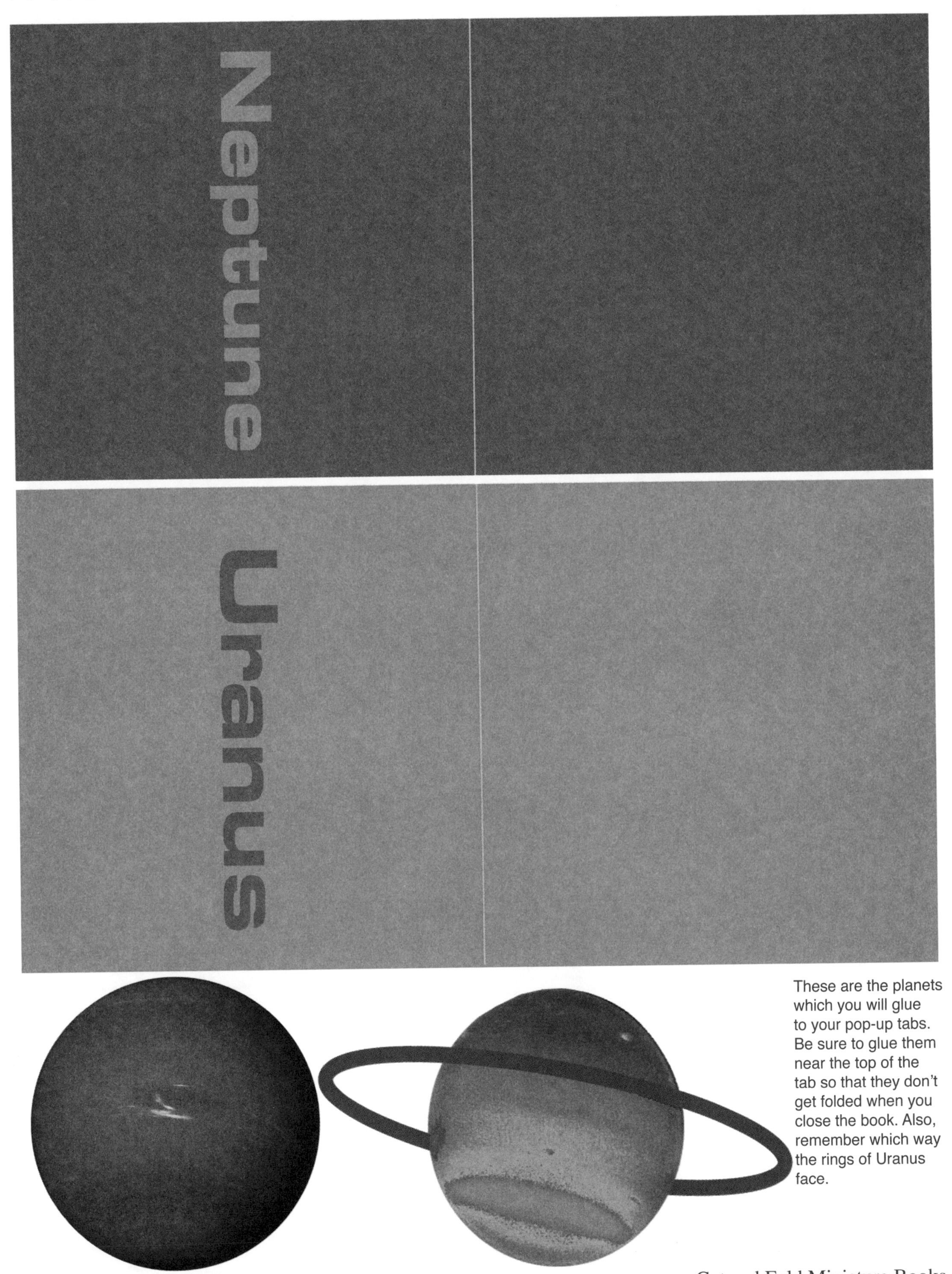

These are the planets which you will glue to your pop-up tabs. Be sure to glue them near the top of the tab so that they don't get folded when you close the book. Also, remember which way the rings of Uranus face.

PLUTO DEBATE MINI BOOK

Instructions:

1. Cut out the two rectangles on this page along the dotted lines. **Do not cut the grey fold lines! Note the instructions on the back of this page for cutting out the small rectangle.**
2. Fold each rectangle in half along the solid grey lines making sure that the "Is Pluto a Planet?" words are on the outside. This rectangle will be your cover page.
3. Place the lined pages inside the cover page and staple them in the center of the book. This will be the booklet in which you will create your Pluto mini book described at the end of lesson 12 (p. 139) of your astronomy text.
4. Glue this side down onto the "Pluto & the Kuiper Belt" paste page.

Instructions:

1. Cut out this small book and fold it in half with Kuiper Belt facing outward.
2. Write down what you learned about the Kuiper belt on the inside.
3. Glue this side of the book to your paste page.

STAR FAN

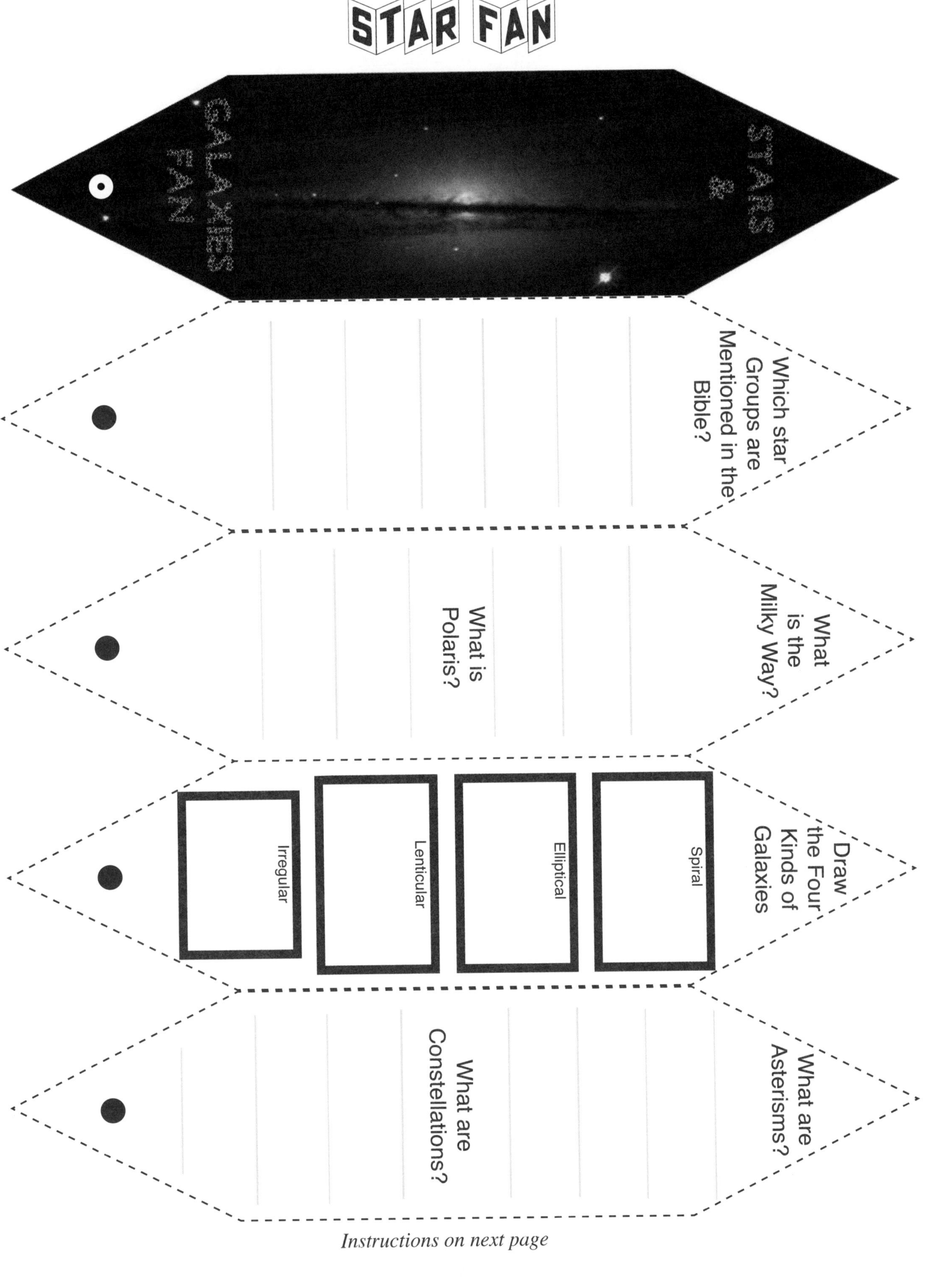

Instructions on next page

What is a Supergiant Star?

What is a Binary Star?

What is a Supernova?

What is a Nebula?

What is a Black Hole?

Instructions:

1. Cut out each individual fan sheet (on this page and the previous).
2. Punch a hole in the bottom of each fan sheet on the black dot.
3. Fill in the information requested under each topic.
4. Stack your fan sheets with the Stars and Galaxies Fan Pocket sheet on top.
5. Secure the fan sheets at the bottom by inserting a brass fastener into the punch hole.
6. Cut out the pocket to the left.
7. Put glue on the bottom and side edges and paste the pocket onto your "Stars and Galaxies" paste page.
8. Place your Star Fan in the pocket and remove it when you want to read all about Stars and Galaxies.

SPACE TRAVEL LIFT AND LOOK

Instructions:

1. Cut out the earth image above. Make small openings in the earth along the white lines.
2. Turn the earth over and place glue around the outer edges. **Be certain not to glue the white openings closed!**
3. Glue the earth image to your "Space Travel" paste page.
4. Cut out each Space Travel shape (on the next two pages).
5. Answer the questions related to each picture.
6. Insert all the shapes except the astronaut into the openings on the earth and slide them down.
7. Insert the astronaut into the middle, and fold face down at the opening. Then fold him upward at the bottom of his boots to make him pop out and wave to you when you open your journal.
8. Pull up each shape to learn about space travel.

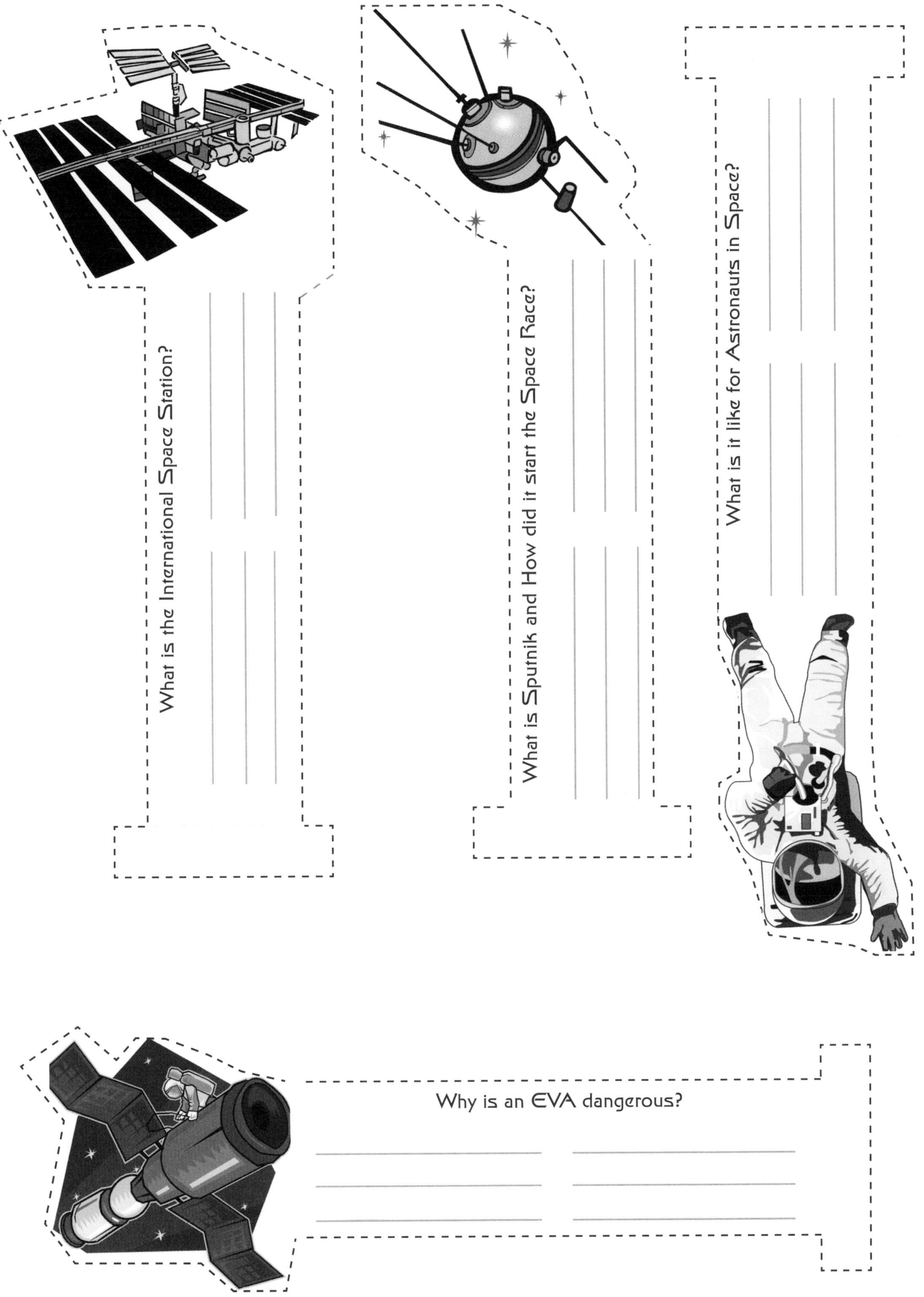
What is the International Space Station?
What is Sputnik and How did it start the Space Race?
What is it like for Astronauts in Space?
Why is an EVA dangerous?

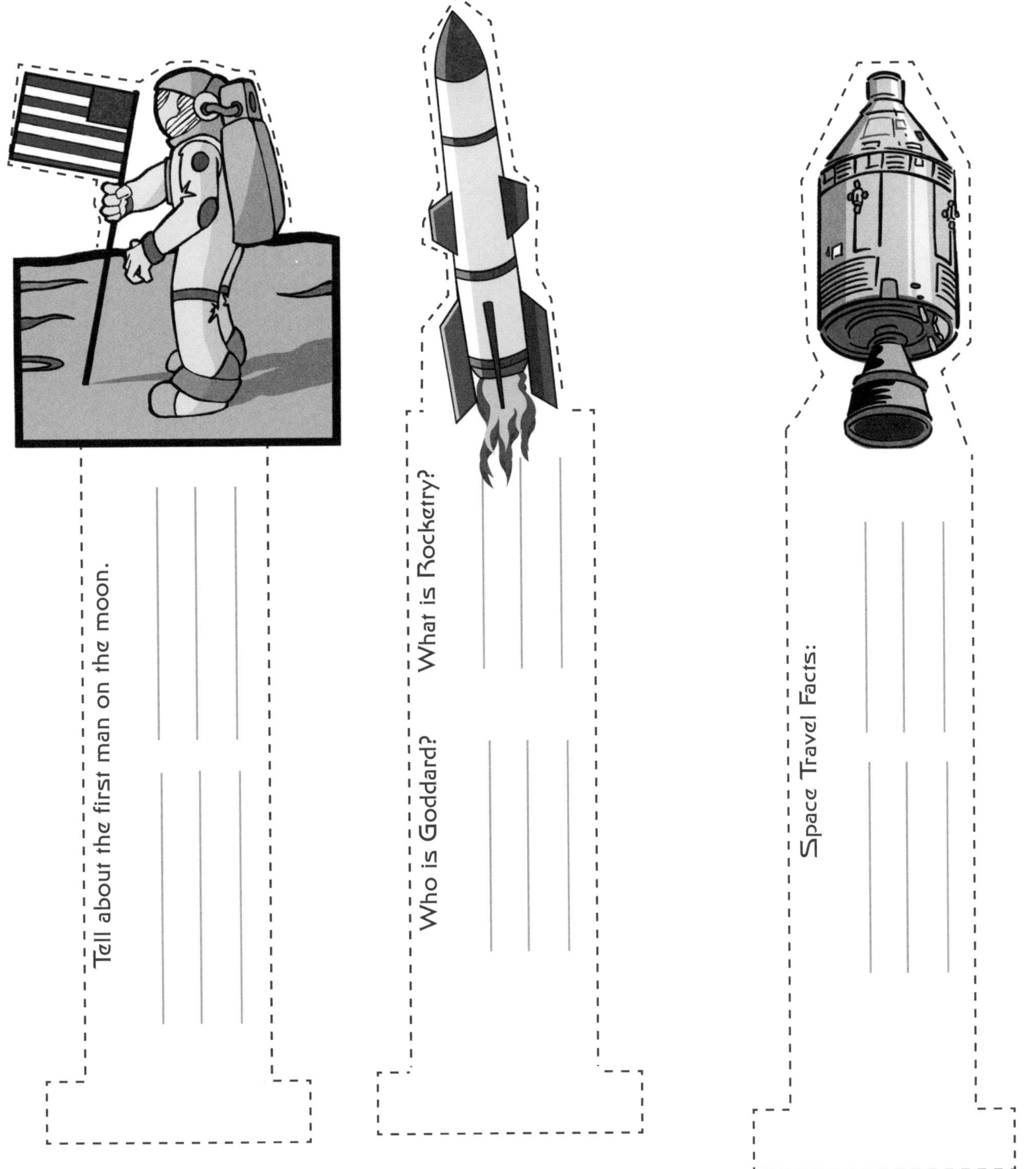
Tell about the first man on the moon.
Who is Goddard?
What is Rocketry?
Space Travel Facts:

SOLAR SYSTEM REVIEW WHEEL

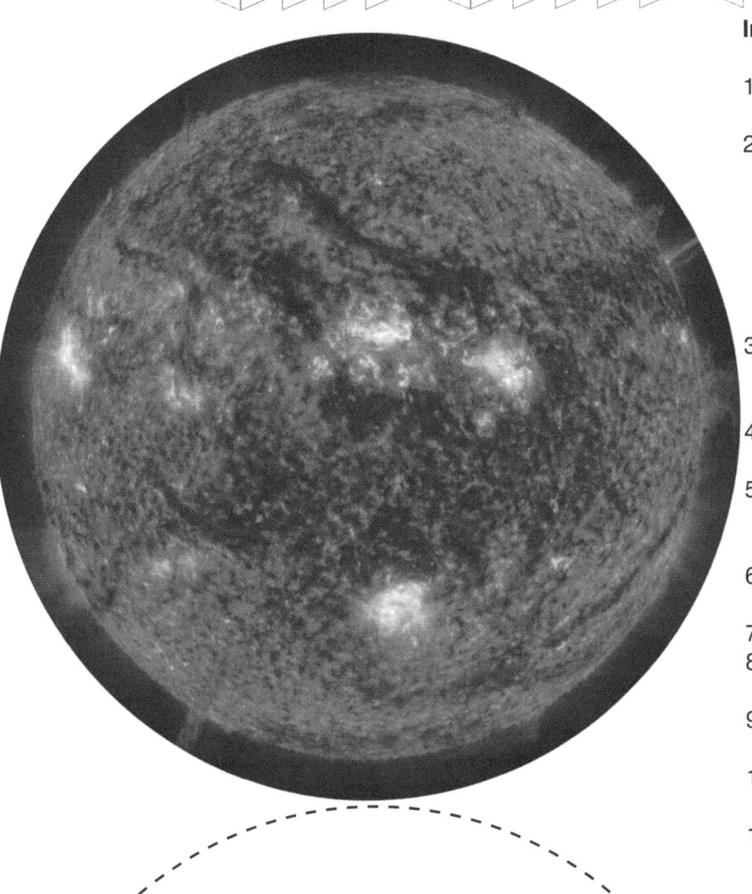

Instructions:

1. Cut out the three circles on this page and the satellite strips on the next page.
2. Write a fact you learned about each planet on the satellite strips. For example, you might write: ***"Called the Red Planet"*** on the strip below the picture of Mars. **Write the fact on the strip as close to the planet as possible, because the bottom half of Mercury, Venus and Earth will be hidden behind the sun when the wheel is assembled.**
3. Punch holes through all the black dots using a hole puncher. You will need to fold down one edge of the circle to get the hole puncher to the center black dot.
4. Place a brass fastener through the hole in the center of Circle 1.
5. Place all the planets behind Circle 1 by placing the fastener through the holes on each strip. Mercury will be the first planet and Neptune will be the last.
6. Place Circle 2 behind the planets by placing the fastener through the circle's hole.
7. Bend down the prongs of your brass fastener.
8. Glue the Sun Circle to the front of Circle 1, on top of the metal fastener head.
9. Glue the back of Circle 2 to the "Planets Review" paste page.
10. When the satellites are fanned out, your wheel will look like the small picture below.
11. Rotate the satellites so that they are above the sun before you close your book.

Circle 2

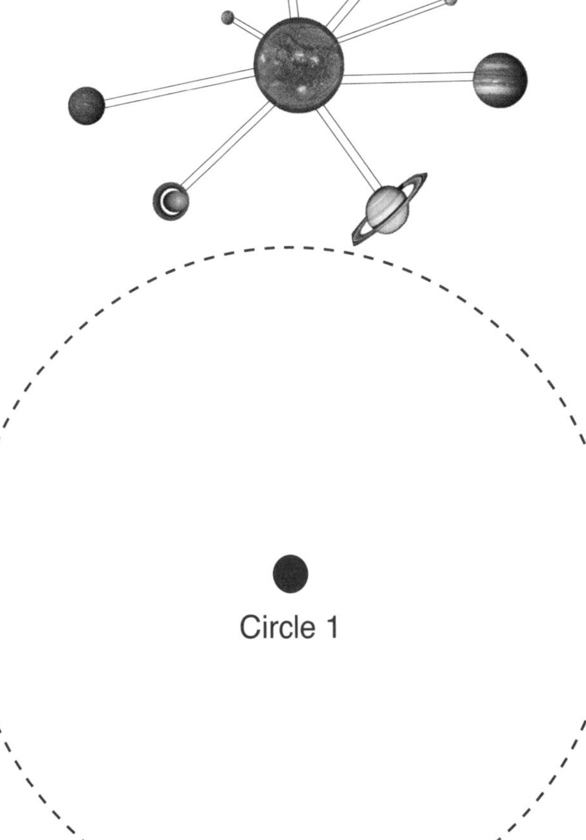